SEP 1 9 2023

Parallel Views

Parallel Views

Education and Access for Deaf People in France and the United States

The French-American Foundation

Introduction by Harlan Lane

Gallaudet University Press / *Washington, D.C.*

Gallaudet University Press
Washington, DC 20002

© 1994 by Gallaudet University. All rights reserved
Published 1994
Printed in the United States of America

Library of Congress Cataloging-in-Publication Data
Parallel views : education and access for deaf people in France and the United States /
The French-American Foundation ; with an introduction by Harlan Lane.
p.   cm.
Includes bibliographical references (p.   ) and index.
ISBN 1-56368-030-0 (acid-free paper)
1. Deaf—Education—France—Congresses.   2. Deaf—Education—United States—
Congresses.   3. Deaf—Services for—France—Congresses.   4. Deaf—Services for—
United States—Congresses.   5. Deaf—France—Social conditions—Congresses.
6. Deaf—United States—Social conditions—Congresses.   I. French-American
Foundation.
HV2735.P37   1994
371.91'2'0944—dc20   94-13471
                                                                                          CIP

*To the deaf communities of France
and the United States*

Contents

Interpreting for Deaf and Hearing People

Education for Deaf Children

The Late-Deafened Person

Preface and Acknowledgments

These articles originated as papers presented at a French-American colloquium, "Deaf People in Society: Education and Access," held in Paris in October of 1991. The colloquium was sponsored by the French-American Foundation, USA, and the Fondation Franco-Américaine, France.

Contributors to this volume have used a variety of terms to designate deaf people. Translations from the French frequently refer to "the deaf." Some American authors use the word "deaf" only as an adjective, while others distinguish between "Deaf" and "deaf"—the former designating members of Deaf culture, the latter referring generally to people with hearing loss. The same varying practices can be found in many recent works concerning deaf people; consequently, we have chosen to respect each author's usage in the absence of a clear (and binational) consensus.

We would like to express our appreciation to Marceau Long, Chairman of the Fondation Franco-Américaine, France, and to Edward Tuck, President of the French-American Foundation, USA. A special thanks to Michel Jaoul, Vice Chairman and President of the Paris Fondation Franco-Américaine for his vision, cooperation, and tireless efforts to make the colloquium become a reality.

We would like to thank the following individuals, without whose support the colloquium would not have been possible: Diantha Schull, former Executive Director of the French-American Foundation, USA; Harlan Lane, Distinguished University Professor at Northeastern University; Harry Markowicz, Assistant Professor at Gallaudet University; Bernard Mottez, Research Director, French National Center for Scientific Research (Centre National de la Recherche Scientifique); and I. King Jordan, President of Gallaudet University. We would also like to acknowledge the late Eli Savanick, Director of the International Center on Deafness at Gallaudet University, for his efforts on behalf of deaf and hearing people in France and the United States.

For their efforts in conceptualizing and implementing the colloquium, we would like to thank the members of the American Scientific Committee and the French Scientific Committee for the colloquium. The members of the American Scientific Committee were Carol Erting, Charles Estes, Harlan Lane, Harry Markowicz, Carol Padden, Diantha Schull, Michael Schwartz, and Sharon Neumann Solow. The members of the French Scientific Committee were Patrick Belissen, Jean-Pierre Bouillon, Nancy Breitenbach, Christian Cuxac, Francis Delhom, Michel Jaoul, Patrick Monod-Gayraud, and Bernard Mottez. For coordinating interpretation in five languages, we would like to thank Sharon Neumann Solow and Rachid Mimoun.

Harlan Lane was instrumental in bringing this project to fruition in its published form, for which we are especially grateful. We are particularly pleased that this book is being published by Gallaudet University Press, under the auspices of the only liberal arts university for deaf people in the United States. We would like to thank Ivey Pittle Wallace, Managing Editor of the Gallaudet University Press, and for their work as technical editors, we would like to thank William Zeisel and Alexa Selph.

We would also like to thank Joan Challinor, Trustee of the French-American Foundation, USA, for her efforts to procure funding for Gallaudet University to continue work in the area of increased understanding between the deaf communities of France and the United States.

Regina Fodor
Director
French-American Foundation, USA

Parallel Views

Introduction

Constructing Deafness in France and the United States

HARLAN LANE

Two Views of Deafness

"When deafness is total, it is a catastrophe." So writes Claude-Henri Chouard, former head of otorhinolaryngology at Paris's prestigious Saint Antoine hospital, and leader in the development of cochlear prostheses for surgical implantation in deaf children and adults.[1] Yet, "It's dandy to be deaf," states Roslyn Rosen, former president of the U.S. National Association of the Deaf, in a jocular tone. Rosen, scion of a distinguished deaf family, mother of two deaf lawyers and a deaf engineer, and author of an article on the politics of deafness in this volume, is vice-president for academic affairs of Gallaudet University.

Both commentators are making claims whose purpose is persuasion. Frequently, their competing claims are addressed to the same groups: parents of deaf children, legislators, and professional people. They speak on behalf of quite different constituencies, however: hearing professionals on the one hand, the deaf community on the other. The two claims-makers would agree, at least, on this: deaf is different. Indeed, the presence of a deaf community among us probes how far we are prepared to go in accepting a minority whose language and culture arise from a physical organization different from our own. It was the opinion of many at the 1991 Paris conference, "Deaf People in Society: Education and Access," from which this volume arose, that

Harlan Lane is Distinguished University Professor at Northeastern University in Boston, Massachusetts.

French society is not prepared to go very far in accepting the deaf difference. French deaf leader Patrick Belissen says it clearly in this volume: "[There is a] mental block vis-à-vis the language and culture of the deaf in institutions charged with serving them [in France]." The Paris conference bore eloquent witness to this state of affairs. Americans who addressed the meeting were primarily deaf people directing professional or governmental programs serving deaf people. A clear common message in their talks was the importance of self-determination, programs "of, by, and for the deaf," as California deaf leader Marcella Meyer put it. French speakers at the head of professional and government programs, however, were commonly hearing; they undertook to describe what France is doing for its deaf citizens. Their attitude toward deaf people seemed patronizing and paternalistic (see the article by Exertier), all the more so as not one senior French official with authority in deaf affairs was on the program, a fact protested from the podium repeatedly by French deaf delegates.

True, the struggle for acceptance of American Sign Language (ASL) is hardly over in the United States; far from it. Nevertheless, numerous states have passed laws affirming that ASL study meets requirements for the study of a foreign language in the high schools; more than a thousand colleges offer ASL classes for credit; American deaf students can attend some two hundred college programs where sign language is used in the classroom. On the other hand, la Langue des Signes Françaises (LSF) has been so downtrodden in France that it took Americans working with French deaf adults to launch the first LSF classes (see J. Bouchauveau). While there are more than one hundred programs in the United States granting academic degrees in interpreter education (see Watson), there is not a single such program in France. Professional interpreter Christiane Fournier affirms that in France the designation "deaf and dumb has a highly negative connotation that conveys the image of a person with a handicap and with low intellectual ability." Indeed, French deaf education is for the most part under the auspices of the French Ministry of Health. The problem, explains deaf leader Rachid Mimoun, president of a French interpreters' organization, is that "the profession cannot develop until the deaf are recognized as having their own culture and their own language." French sociologist Bernard Mottez sums it up: "Sign language is a fact of life in the United States. . . . We in France are far from having reached that stage."

Instead, the order of the day in French schools is spoken French (commonly called oralism when applied to deaf children). Since nine out of ten deaf children today were born deaf or became so before they could master an oral language, education that tries to use spoken language crowds out all other instruction and ultimately fails.[2] "Despite all the efforts of speech therapists," Professor Chouard notes, most French deaf children "scarcely know how to speak" (p. 7). "Many children wear their hearing aids only in school because they are obliged to, while setting them aside at home, because they are of no help" (p. 7). French deaf adults are often deeply marked, not to say scarred, by these educational practices; that is why, for example, French deaf leader Jean-François Mercurio took a sledgehammer to a hearing aid in front of the media at the opening of a 1990 international conference on sign language in Poitiers. While some ten thousand American deaf students are currently enrolled in college (see article by Watson), and there is a substantial American deaf middle class including many professional people, French children who have grown up deaf rarely complete regular high school,[3] not to mention college and the professions; instead they are shunted into vocational training (see Morel). Generally speaking, it seems that French society, profoundly convinced that deafness is a catastrophe, acts to make it so.

Common sense rebels; this indictment of the French approach to deafness seems to stand matters on their head: deafness isn't a catastrophe because the French think so; rather, the French think so because deafness is indeed a catastrophe. However, the American deaf point of view is troubling for this commonsense position; how can Gallaudet Vice-President Rosen say, "Deaf is dandy"; how can a deaf school superintendent like Gertrude Galloway state sincerely, "It is okay to be deaf" (see article in this volume). Comparisons of views of social problems across cultures, like those across time within a culture, reveal that social problems can be construed in various ways.

Social Problems Are Constructed

Consider a few brief examples of the varying constructions of social problems. First, alcoholism. It is generally recognized that sufferers from alcoholism need specially trained people to help them—alcoholism counselors, psychologists, and psychiatrists; they need special facilities such as detoxification centers; and special organizations like Alcoholics Anonymous. However, this understanding of alcoholism is less than fifty years old. Recall that the American Temperance Movement of the last century viewed excessive drinking not as a disease but as an act of will; the solution was the prohibition of sales. Some groups favored prohibition and took the moral high ground; other groups felt justified in breaking the law. Special facilities existed then to house and treat many problem groups—mentally ill people, for example—but not people who drank too much. Only recently has a consensus developed that excessive drinking is a disease—a matter of individual suffering more than a political dispute. With this shift in the construction of alcoholism, the evident need was for medical research to alleviate suffering; vast sums of money are now devoted to research on alcoholism, and there is now a large treatment establishment with halfway houses, hospital wards, outpatient clinics, and specialized hospitals.[4]

Consider another example: the "discovery" of child abuse dates from the 1950s. Radiologists and pediatricians first decried the evidence they were seeing of parents beating their children. The Children's Bureau, a government agency, and the media took up the cause (it is still very present in TV and the newspapers) and made the public aware of this social problem. In the decade that followed, the states passed laws requiring reports of child abuse and providing penalties. Of course, parents did not start beating their children only in the 1950s. Rather, a social consensus emerged in that decade that a problem existed requiring laws, special welfare workers, and special budgetary provisions. In the last century, the major problems associated with children concerned poverty and child labor—a rather different and much more political construction of the problem of improper treatment of children.[5]

Mental retardation was first presented as a public menace requiring social measures such as isolating this group in institutions and sterilizing its members to prevent their procreation. Later, the problem of mental retardation was recast as a problem with individuals, most of them trainable or educable, who required welfare services. More recently, mentally retarded people are presented as an oppressed minority group; many retarded people, it is argued, have suffered needlessly from welfare services that without realizing it judged their clients by middle-class norms and found them lacking.[6]

For a long time, the dominant construction of homosexuality, like that of alcoholism, was a moral one: men and women were making sinful choices; the problem was "owned" by the church. Later, psychiatry gave it a new construction: it was an illness, they claimed, that psychiatrists could treat. In the third phase, homosexuals are now presented as a minority group; they ask for the same protection as all other groups that are discriminated against based on the circumstances of their birth, such as blacks and women.[7]

Social problems, it seems, are partly what we make of them; they are not just out there "lying in the road to be discovered by passersby."[8] The particular way in which society understands alcoholism, or child abuse, or mental retardation, or homosexuality determines exactly what these labels mean, how large groups of people are treated, and the problems that they face. Deafness, too, has many constructions; they differ with time and place. Where there were many deaf people in small communities in the last century, on the island of Martha's Vineyard, for example, deafness was apparently not seen as a problem requiring special intervention. Most Americans had quite a different construction of deafness at that time, however: it was an individual affliction that befell family members and had to be accommodated within the family. The great challenge facing New England pastor Thomas Gallaudet and the deaf French educator Laurent Clerc was to persuade state legislatures and wealthy Americans of quite a different construction, which Gallaudet and Clerc had learned in France: deafness was not an individual but a social problem; deaf people had to be brought together for their instruction, special "asylums" were needed. Nowadays, two constructions of deafness in particular are dominant and compete for shaping deaf peoples' destinies. The one construes "deaf" as designating a category of disability; the other construes "deaf" as designating a member of a linguistic and cultural minority.

The struggle between groups adhering to these two contrasting constructions has persisted across the centuries in part because there is no simple criterion for identifying most candidates as clients of one position or the other. Each construction has a core client group. No one disputes the claim of the hearing adult become deaf from illness or aging that he or she is disabled and not a member of deaf culture. Nor, on the other hand, has anyone yet criticized deaf parents for insisting that their deaf child has a distinct linguistic and cultural heritage. More generally, we can observe that late deafening and moderate hearing loss tend to be associated with the disability construction of deafness while early and profound deafness involves the entire organization of the person's language, culture, and thought around vision and tends to be associated with the linguistic minority construction.

In the disability construction, deafness is associated with silence, the absence of hearing, individual suffering, personal incapacities, and achievement in overcoming great obstacles. In the cultural minority construction, deafness is associated with a unique language, history, culture, social group, and set of social institutions.

LSF and French Ethnocentrism

Thus, "total catastrophe" and "dandy" reflect two different constructions of deafness; both are promoted by claims-making groups in France and in America. However, the balance between these two constructions is different, I would argue, in our two societies: the "catastrophe" construction predominates more in France. This conclusion is disheartening, all the more so when we recall that France was the cradle of Western deaf education; that more sign languages in the world today trace their roots to LSF than to any other sign language; and that American deaf leaders revere the French for having established the network of American residential schools for the deaf, the land of this nation without a country (to paraphrase Bernard Mottez).

If we acknowledge that the balance of "catastrophe" and "culture" constructions of deafness is different in France and America, the question arises as to whether this difference in balance is shaped by some underlying difference in our two societies. Since we are examining the acceptance of a cultural construction, surely we must consider the place for cultural diversity in French society.

But is it possible in the first place to generalize usefully about differences in our two societies? Each contrast seems to be embedded in a host of other detailed differences. Thus, in order to make a point (about cultural constructions), I have contrasted culturally deaf students' access to college in the United States with their lockout in France. It is, however, commonly acknowledged that the French *baccalauréat* is more academically demanding than the American high school diploma. The two kinds of secondary education have quite different histories, are staffed by professionals with quite different training and qualifications, and teach student bodies that are differently constituted. Likewise, the two countries differ in the roles that deaf organizations and parents have played in deaf education. At the postsecondary level, there are many programs and schools in the United States designed for deaf students (Gallaudet University is perhaps the most famous); these schools recruit deaf students in order to accomplish their mission, and they admit some with limited literacy; they underrecruit blacks and Hispanics (Dunn). All these specifics— historical and social embedding, if you will, of the phenomenon under study—enrich the description of what it is that invites explanation; and they constrain possible explanations; but they are not the explanations themselves. For that we must turn to a wider frame of reference. I turn here to the place made for cultural diversity in the structures of each society.

"FRENCH LANGUAGE" cried a front-page headline in the *Figaro* in 1993. And a box explains: "We didn't know how to mobilize to save French." The article continues on the front page of the second section and invites the reader's horror at the mixing of English and French in such subversive billboard advertising as "The pastis, né in the country of the cigale." For many Americans, a Frenchman can no more be separated from pride in French language and culture than from a penchant for cuisine and public displays of affection— French ethnocentrism is a source of humor for commentators, frustration for politicians, and anecdotes for travelers; its origins predate the founding of the first French Republic.

During the French Enlightenment, an evolutionary theory of language held sway; according to Condillac, the primitive basis for all languages was gestural language; with civilization, increasing refinement of language took place, culminating in the French of the capital.[9] The *Encyclopedia* defined a patois as "a degenerate tongue such as is spoken in almost all the provinces. . . . The language of France is spoken only in the capital."[10] Indeed, endorsing a claim of the Port-Royal grammarians a half-century earlier, Diderot affirmed that French corresponds to human logic, as the order of words in French corresponds to their natural order in the mind.[11]

From its birth in 1789, the new nation felt threatened by the diversity of languages within its borders, all the more so as some of these languages were spoken across its borders by its enemies. Abbé Grégoire, a member of the Committee of Public Instruction and possibly the best-known "patriot curate" of revolutionary France, was instructed by the legislature to conduct a massive investigation of the "patois" spoken in various regions of France. His report, *On the Necessity and Means of Destroying the Patois and Universalizing the Use of French*, revealed that far fewer than half of all "Frenchmen" were native speakers of French, and that roughly one-half could not understand the language of the Revolution. "Governments do not realize, or do not feel keenly enough," Grégoire exhorted, "how much the annihilation of regional speech is necessary for education, the true knowledge of religion, the ready implementation of the law, national happiness and political tranquility."[12] "Federalism and superstition speak Breton," the legislature was told. "Emigration and hate of the republic speak German; the counterrevolution speaks Italian and fanaticism speaks Basque."[13]

Shortly after Grégoire's report, speaking German, for example, was banned in Alsace—tantamount to telling most Alsatians not to speak at all. The legislature further created primary schools where all children would learn French, and only French would be used in instruction.[14]

In 1779, in what may be the first book published by a deaf person, Pierre Desloges assailed the practice of forcing deaf children to try to speak French; prohibiting deaf children from using French Sign Language, he objected, was tantamount to prohibiting them from speaking at all. At the same time, the Abbé de l'Epée was promoting the education of the deaf through a manual code based on French, in which signs were assigned to every prefix, suffix, root, conjunction, preposition, and article in French, to be executed in French word order. Epée's successor, Sicard, held on to the cumbrous French code, for his pupils' untutored natural language was lower even than a patois in his eyes: "We all know the kinds of sentences in use among the Negro tribes," he wrote, "but those used by the deaf and dumb are even closer to nature, even more primitive." [15] It mattered not a whit that Pierre Desloges had given a ringing defense of LSF in his book a decade earlier, showing how it served the needs of the deaf community of Paris, so that "no event in Paris, in France, or in the four corners of the world lies outside the scope of their discussions." [16] Had not Napoleon exclaimed to Sicard that sign language had only nouns and adjectives? [17] And Sicard's colleague Jean-Marc Itard, founder of French otology, vilified French Sign Language as "that barbaric language without pronouns, without conjunctions, without any of the words that permit us to express abstract ideas." [18]

In the following decades, LSF did gain a temporary foothold within the schools for deaf children in France. It was however, constantly under attack and frequently banned in favor of the exclusive use of French. [19] The fear of linguistic diversity had not diminished in France eight decades after the Revolution, even though the new institutions had become secure. In 1864, the minister of public instruction repeated the Grégoire investigation. "Are there schools in your sector where instruction is in the patois?" he wrote to public school inspectors in the provinces. "What can be done to change this state of affairs?" [20]

What could be done about the indigenous language in the schools for deaf children was decided definitively in a series of stage-managed congresses of hearing educators of the deaf. The first was hastily convened in Paris, at the French Exposition of 1878, by a small group of French educators who advocated teaching deaf children using spoken French. The self-styled "international congress" affirmed the importance of French in deaf education, and scheduled a larger meeting to be held two years later in Italy, which was just emerging from a period of unification, the Risorgimento. At the infamous Milan congress, which called for a worldwide ban on signed languages, the delegates from France and Italy comprised seven-eighths of the membership. The French government, complying with the Milan resolutions, banished LSF from public education of its deaf children and fired all deaf teachers, on the grounds that they would be likely to use LSF. Shortly thereafter, the government banished all minority languages from all its schools, decreeing the schools free, monolingual, and compulsory until age thirteen.

By the turn of the century, the colonial adventure and the forced assimilation of vast regions of Africa and Asia had superseded the forced assimilation of Breton, Basque, and Occitan a century earlier. Whereas some colonizing powers, such as the English in Africa, imposed their language on subjugated peoples while tolerating the indigenous languages in education, art, and other fields, the French generally sought exclusive use of French, particularly in the schools. Moreover, French African territories were divided up in such a way that larger language groups crossed boundaries; the diversity of languages within each territory, then, favored the imposition of French as lingua franca.

Although most former French colonies had gained their independence by the 1960s, French activism for "defense and promotion of the French language" had not diminished, and the French government created a commission with that name and mission in 1966. Four years later, it also created a government agency for economic cooperation among twenty-five French-speaking nations; both are still active today. The colonial and neocolonial argument that the French make for their language is two-pronged: First, French is one of the world's great languages, with the resources in grammar, vocabulary, and texts to enable those who otherwise speak a restricted local idiom to gain access to the world's store of knowledge, its corridors of power, and its boardrooms of commerce. Second, the native idioms cannot fulfill these functions. Similarly, the discourse of French educators of the deaf contends that "the world will never learn LSF," and LSF, they reassure one another, can never fulfill the functions of French. Echoing Napoleon's exclamation to Abbé Sicard, a modern French educator has written of LSF: "Mimic [*sic*] grammar is characterized above all by simplifications. No articles; adverbs and adjectives are indistinguishable"[21]

In view of the slice of cultural and political history traced summarily here, it is hardly any wonder that French administration and law view culturally deaf people, most of whose parents are monoculturally French, less as a linguistic minority and more as members of a larger group of disabled French-speaking citizens. Moreover, the self-interest of most of the concerned bureaucracies and professions, run by hearing people in France, lies in institutionalizing the need for their ever-expanding services; and this favors strengthening the disability construction (see Exertier).[22] When Dr. Chouard tells us that total deafness is "a catastrophe," that "it brings with it severe intellectual impairment," (p. 5) and that "the child born deaf ... gradually comes to resemble an animal," he is not merely endorsing the commonsense construction of deafness as disability, he is also positioning his profession to intervene with life-changing surgery of unproven value and unassessed risk for deaf children. In contemporary French society, the pursuit of spoken French is worth any price.

Counterevidence from Deaf Affairs

While it may be true that a disability construction of deafness predominates over a cultural one by a larger margin in France than in the United States, the influence of the American "troubled-persons industry" in promoting a disability construction of culturally deaf children and adults is enormous. Many developments in France, on the other hand, promise the strengthening of the cultural construction there. The American government has approved cochlear implant surgery on deaf children down to the age of two and funds numerous surgical implant "teams," although the National Association of the Deaf has decried the surgery and rehabilitation as "unsound scientifically, procedurally, and ethically."[23] The American medical and paramedical establishment, like the French, views all deafness as a catastrophe that urgently demands their early and prolonged intervention.

Moreover, Americans can take little satisfaction from the conduct of deaf education in the United States, despite the growing acceptance of deaf culture and the increasing use of ASL in recent decades. In its testimony in 1992 to a legislative committee, the National Association of the Deaf (NAD) affirmed that there is "a national crisis in the education of deaf and hard of hearing children in the United States"[24] and went on to list numerous unmet educational needs of American deaf children, as follows: They need appropriate early intervention so that they receive full access to language; they need valid tests of their strengths and weaknesses; they must have access to top-quality residential schools, and no deaf child should be isolated in a classroom with few or no other deaf children; deaf pupils need teachers and other professionals who can communicate with them fluently; they need support services that work, including qualified interpreters. To meet many of these needs, the field of deaf education must do much more than is being done at present to improve the training and hiring of deaf professionals as teachers, counselors, and administrators at every educational level.

French legislation passed in 1991 gives language choice to parents of deaf children, including the right to elect education for their children conducted in LSF and French, or in French alone (see Reynaud, Bouillon). The U.S. government, on the other hand, has ignored the recommendation of the Congressional Commission on the Education of the Deaf that federal programs supporting bilingual education should include schools with large numbers of ASL-speaking children.[25] Such schools, moreover, are becoming rare in the United States, where the vogue of academic integration has led to the isolation of most deaf children in hearing classrooms with only one or two deaf children and an uncommunicative teacher.[26] Few American deaf people teach in the programs for deaf children that remain (see Markowicz).[27] French deaf educators, on the other hand, pioneered bilingual/bicultural education of deaf children (see Brusque), a movement just now gaining impetus in the United States (see Reynolds). Nevertheless, the French law promising bilingual education for LSF-speaking children remains just a promise; it has yet to be implemented, and it is unclear how it can be implemented on a large scale, given the traditional barriers to deaf people found in French education.

Some French universities have begun providing basic services for deaf students so that they are not effectively locked out (see Barth). Yet few members of the deaf community attend those universities. Community members are increasingly providing professional services to deaf people, as mental health workers (see Karakostas), as museum tour guides and instructors (see G. Bouchauveau), and as teachers' aides and as teachers (see Abbou). Moreover, deaf leaders have been actively advancing the field of deaf history in France.[28] However, French deaf people have for the most part persevered in these professions without the formal recognition and remuneration that professional diplomas provide (see Abbou).

There are now young interpreter associations in France, while the established ones in the United States have come under fire from the American deaf community (see Rosen). There is also a shortage of interpreters in the United States; if the goal is to provide deaf Americans with the same access to American institutions as their hearing counterparts, then the shortage is astronomical. Still, it is several times worse in France.

There has been broad discussion of the renaissance of American deaf culture in recent decades, heralded by the acknowledgment of ASL as a natural language and marked by the flourishing of the deaf arts, deaf history, ASL instruction and deaf studies, political activism of deaf leaders, anthropological and sociological studies of the deaf community, and unprecedented attention to deaf issues in the media. Before pointing to this renaissance as evidence for the more favorable balance of cultural and disability constructions of deafness in the United States, however, it must be remembered that a similar renaissance has been taking place in France. The French-American conference from which the present volume arose was the latest in a series of developments that may be said to have begun at the 1975 congress in Washington, D.C., of the World Federation of the Deaf.[29] French deaf leaders there were impressed (perhaps overly so) with the place that had been made for ASL in American society. In the same year, French national television started a weekly program aimed at deaf and hard of hearing people and interpreted into sign language. The Fédération Nationale des Sourds de France (the French counterpart of the NAD) launched a study of deaf communication and of the merits of the American system of Total Communication in the classroom.

In 1976, French sociologist Bernard Mottez and American linguist Harry Markowicz, at the French National Scientific Research Center (CNRS) Laboratory for the Study of Social Movements, undertook a study of the growing deaf movement. A year later these scholar-activists began a graduate seminar on the deaf community and a series of public lectures by American deaf scholars such as Gil Eastman, Tom Humphries, I. King Jordan, Barbara Kannapell, Tom Mayes, and Carol Padden. They also began publishing a hard-hitting and insightful "underground newspaper" called *Coup d'Oeil (At a Glance),* which focused on the deaf community and its language. During this period the International Visual Theater, with American deaf director Alfredo Corrado and an all-deaf cast, was founded in Paris at the Chateau de Vincennes; the group presented avant-garde plays in LSF on themes in deaf culture. The high visibility of the theater group inspired respect for LSF among both deaf and hearing audiences. In response to the growing demand for instruction in LSF, the American interpreter for the troupe, Bill Moody, trained troupe members as teachers and established LSF classes at the Chateau for parents and professional people. Four summer institutes at Gallaudet University (in 1978, 1979, 1981, and 1982), organized by Mottez and Markowicz, brought some thirty French parents, professionals, and deaf people each year face-to-face with American hearing and deaf ASL scholars, with politically active deaf groups such as Deafpride, and with the American civil rights movement.

On return to France, one group of deaf participants and hearing allies worked to reclaim French deaf history and to conduct research on LSF; the Academy of French Sign Language was established at "Saint-Jacques," the Paris National Institute for Young Deaf People, and scholars began working on an LSF dictionary and offering classes in LSF. Other graduates of the Gallaudet summer institutes launched a nationwide association committed to the bilingual education of deaf children, *Deux Langues pour Une Education (Two Languages, One Education),* which had its own magazine, *Vivre Ensemble (Living Together),* and conducted summer institutes based on the Gallaudet model. At these institutes, parents and their deaf children, interpreters, and deaf people gathered for mutual instruction. Deaf Americans, such as Gil Eastman, taught workshops there. The association also created bilingual classes for deaf children in several cities. This gave rise, in turn, to regional groups engaged in applied research and development related to LSF—for example, the Association les Iris in Toulouse.

When, in 1985, hearing teachers at the residential school in Poitiers, joined by deaf adults, staged a hunger strike to demand the inclusion of LSF and deaf teachers, they brought the sorry state of deaf education to national attention. A call to deaf people and their friends a year later to rally at the Bastille on behalf of official recognition of LSF resulted in a media event in which three to five thousand people, including legislators and parents, marched through the city to the offices of the prime minister. The march not only enlightened millions of French people but also breathed pride, vigor, and a sense of power into the deaf community of France. Among events reaching the general public, the widely attended French play *Les Enfants du Silence* had a significant role in awakening French society to the linguistic minority in its midst, as did the American play *Children of a Lesser God*, on which it was based.

Several major books on French Sign Language and the French deaf community, as well as a splendid journal of French deaf history, the *Cahiers de l'Histoire des Sourds,* have appeared since the 1970s.[30] As part of the bicentennial of the French Revolution, a magnificent panorama of French deaf history was prepared and placed on display at the Sorbonne.[31] An international conference on signed languages held in Poitiers in July 1990 drew inspiration from the 1988 Gallaudet Deaf President Now Revolution and was in many respects a political gathering to chart a course for reform. In 1991, the present conference was convened, and bilingual education for deaf children was approved by the French Parliament. In 1992, the first European Conference on Deaf History was convened by French deaf organizations in Rodez. And in 1993 *Les Enfants du Silence* began a second run, starring deaf actress Emmanuelle Laborit, who, when she was seven, attended the Gallaudet summer institute with her parents.

The evidence, then, that French deaf people are discriminated against in education, employment, and political life must be judged in the context of these many positive developments in France in recent decades; and any claim that a different balance of constructions of deafness in the United States has led to more progress for deaf people must be considered in the light of all the social injustices still heaped on deaf Americans.

Counterevidence in the Context
of Broader Social Issues

If it is true that a disability construction of deafness predominates more over a cultural one in France than in the United States, this may reflect not so much differences in the tolerance of diversity in the two cultures as a difference in beliefs about how minorities can achieve social justice. In the French view, a democracy without institutionalized cultural distinctions is more just; many Americans also hold this view and claim, for example, that fair laws are "color-blind." For the French, to give everyone equal educational opportunity is to give each person equal access in principle to schools conducted in French. Not surprisingly, in view of its history, American society is, on the other hand, more pluralist and more responsive institutionally to what minorities state is in their own interest; and language minorities generally put the preservation of their language high in their priorities. Acting through the courts and through law-making bodies, those minorities have won the right to instruction using their languages in U.S. schools.

And while it may be true that French ethnocentrism underlies the predisposition toward a disability construction of deafness, the American melting pot is stirred vigorously by monoculturalist forces. A large and growing movement for "English First" has made important gains on the state and federal levels.[32] Court-ordered and congressionally legislated programs of bilingual education in the United States generally do not embrace diversity. Their goal is the assimilation of children from minority cultures; their means include tolerating the child's primary language for a while. It is an empirical question whether a language minority's education is best advanced by refusing or by using its language in the schools; the abundant research has been hotly disputed, although, on balance, it favors bilingual education.[33] In the end, many would say there is no sound basis for choosing between the French monocultural approach to social justice and the more pluralistic approach in the United States. There is, however, one group of people who indisputably cannot get social justice in schools that use only the national language, and that is children who use sign language; most such children are deaf, so—unlike their hearing counterparts—they are bound to drown with total immersion in the national oral language; and drown they do.[34]

The difference in pluralism between the United States and France is not so much in demographics as in the pluralism of government structures. France is, after all, a pluralistic society; numerous French citizens speak as their primary language Arabic, Turkish, Vietnamese, or LSF, to mention just a few languages. French people differ in their regional affiliations, cultural origins, social classes, and political parties. However, until recently in France, as sociologist Dominique Schnapper writes, "there was no place for the constitution of ethnic groups intervening as such in French political life. . . . The school system took no account of what was unique about the children of immigrants." (see Mottez).[35] France has long wanted to overlook the fact that it is a country with immigrants. "It sheltered foreigners but acknowledged Frenchmen."[36] However, things have changed in the last fifteen years, she maintains. Both the social sciences and political life are restructuring themselves in ways favorable to cultural pluralism. Perhaps the passage of the law granting parents of deaf children a language choice reflects this growing tolerance of cultural diversity. In the next few years, the cultural construction of deafness may well blossom in France, not merely reducing the contrast with the United States, but implementing the aspirations of culturally deaf people in entirely novel ways.[37]

Notes

1. C.-H. Chouard, *Entendre sans oreille* (Paris: Laffont, 1978), 21.

2. The figures are based on American surveys and may not be accurate for France. See S. C. Brown "Etiological Trends, Characteristics, and Distributions," in *Deaf Children in America*, ed. A. N. Schildroth and M. A. Karchmer (San Diego, Calif.: College-Hill, 1986), 33–54.

3. C. Cuxac, "La langue des signes: Construction d'un objet scientifique," *Psychoanalyses* 46–47 (1993): 98.

4. This discussion follows J. Gusfield, "Deviance in the Welfare State: The Alcoholism Profession and the Entitlements of Stigma," in *Research in Social Problems and Public Policy*, vol 2, ed. M. Lewis (Greenwich, Conn.: JAI press, 1982), 8ff.

5. J. Gusfield, "Constructing the Ownership of Social Problems: Fun and Profit in the Welfare State," *Social Problems* 36 (1989), 436.

6. J. Carrier, "Special Education and the Explanation of Pupil Performance," *Disability, Handicap and Society* 5 (1990), 214.

7. See the historical account in P. Conrad and J. Schneider, *Deviance and Medicalization: From Badness to Sickness* (Columbus: Merrill, 1980).

8. J. Gusfield, "On the Side: Practical Action and Social Constructivism in Social Problems Theory," in *Studies in the Sociology of Social Problems*, ed. J. Schneider and J. Kitsuse (Norwood, N.J.: Ablex, 1984), 38.

9. E. B. Condillac, *Major Philosophical Works of Etienne Bonnot de Condillac*, trans. H. Lane and F. Philip (Hillsdale, N.J.: LEA, 1982).

10. D. Diderot (1765), p. 992 of the 1778 ed. Quoted in M. Certeau, D. Julia, and J. Revel, *Une politique de la langue. La Revolution Française et les patois: l'Enquête de Grégoire* (Paris: Gaillard, 1975), 51.

11. D. Diderot, "Lettre sur les sourds et muets" [1751], in *Oeuvres completes*, vol. 1 (Paris: Garnier, 1875), 349–428. Reprinted in *Diderot Studies*, 1965, vol. 7.

12. Grégoire quoted in Certeau, Julia, and Revel, *Une politique de la langue*, 21.

13. *Archives Parlementaires*, series 1, vol. 83 (Paris: Centre National de la Recherche Scientifique, 1961), 715, quoted in Certeau, Julia, and Revel, *Une politique de la langue*, 11.

14. L.-J. Calvet, *Linguistique et colonialisme* (Paris: Payot, 1974), 168. Grégoire's report to the legislature took place on July 30, 1793. On October 21, 1793, the Convention passed a law establishing state primary schools where children would learn French. Five days later, a second decree affirmed that only French should be the language of instruction in those schools. On December 17, 1793, the Committee of Public Safety prohibited the use of German in Alsace.

15. R. A. Sicard, *Second mémoire sur l'art d'instruire les sourds et muets de naissance* (Paris: Knapen, 1790).

16. P. Desloges, "Observations of a deaf-mute," in *The Deaf Experience: Classics in Language and Education*, ed. H. Lane and F. Philip (Cambridge, Mass.: Harvard University Press, 1984).

17. Cited in A. Houdin, *Rapport sur le congrès international des maîtres des sourds-muets à Milan en 1880* (Paris: Imprimerie Nationale, 1881).

18. Cited in A. L. Blanchet, *La Surdi-Mutite* (Paris: Labe, 1850).

19. See H. Lane, *When the Mind Hears: A History of the Deaf* (New York:

Random House, 1984). French trans.: *Quand l'esprit entend* (Paris: Odile Jacob, 1990).

20. *Bulletin Administratif du Ministère de Instruction Publique, nouvelle serie,* 1864, 1, 395–406, quoted in Certeau, Julia, and Revel, *Une politique de la langue,* 270.

21. D. Colin, *Psychologie de l'enfant sourd* (Paris: Masson, 1978), 13.

22. For a discussion of the role of professional interest in promoting the disability construction, see H. Lane, *The Mask of Benevolence: Disabling the Deaf Community* (New York: Knopf, 1992).

23. National Association of the Deaf, Cochlear Implant Task Force, "Cochlear Implants in Children: A Position Paper of the National Association of the Deaf," February 2, 1991. Reprinted in *The National Association of the Deaf Broadcaster* 13 (March 1991): 1.

24. National Association of the Deaf. Testimony: Education of the Deaf Act Reauthorization, House Subcommittee on Select Education, February 25, 1992, p. 1.

25. Commission on Education of the Deaf, *Toward Equality: Education of the Deaf* (Washington, D.C.: Government Printing Office, 1988).

26. Convention of American Instructors of the Deaf, "Schools and Classes for the Deaf in the United States," *American Annals of the Deaf* 138 (1993): 138. S. Foster, "Reflections of a Group of Deaf Adults on Their Experiences in Mainstream and Residential School Programs in the United States," *Disability, Handicap and Society* 4 (1989): 44.

27. H. Lane, *The Mask of Benevolence: Disabling the Deaf Community* (New York: Knopf, 1992).

28. B. Truffaut, "Etienne de Fay and the History of the Deaf," in *Looking Back: A Reader on the History of Deaf Communities and Their Sign Languages,* ed. R. Fischer and H. Lane (Hamburg: Signum, 1993), 13–24. The Colloque Européen sur l'Histoire des Sourds was held in Rodez, France, July 6–12, 1992.

29. This précis is based in part on B. Mottez and H. Markowicz, "The Social Movement for the Acceptance of French Sign Language," in *Sign Language and the Deaf Community. Essays in Honor of William Stokoe,* ed. C. Baker and R. Battison (Silver Spring, Md.: National Association of the Deaf, 1980), 221–232. And on C. Cuxac, "La langue des signes: Construction d'un objet scientifique," *Psychoanalyses* (1993); 46–47, 97–113. Harry Markowicz and Bernard Mottez provided me with much helpful supplementary information.

30. C. Cuxac, *L'Education des sourds en France depuis l'abbé de l'Epée,* Doctorat de Troisième Cycle, Université de Paris V, 1980. Reprinted in *Le langage des sourds* (Paris: Payot, 1983); W. Moody, *Introduction à l'histoire et à la grammaire de la langue des signes. Entre les mains des sourds* (Paris: International Visual Theater, 1983). The *Cahiers de l'histoire des sourds* is published by the Association Etienne de Fay, 46ter rue Ste. Catherine, 4500 Orléans. Also see J. Grémion, *La planète des sourds* (Paris: Messinger, 1990).

31. See the memorial volume, A. Karakostas, ed., *Le Pouvoir des signes* (Paris: Institut National des Jeunes Sourds, 1990).

32. R. P. Porter, *Forked Tongue: The Politics of Bilingual Education* (New York: Basic Books, 1990).

33. R. P. Porter, *Forked Tongue*. T. Skutnabb-Kangas and J. Cummins, *Minority Education* (Philadelphia: Multilingual Matters, 1986). K. Hakuta, *Mirror of Language: The Debate on Bilingualism* (New York: Basic Books, 1986).

34. See H. Lane, *The Mask of Benevolence*.

35. D. Schnapper, "Réflexion critique sur deux concepts de la sociologie Américaine," in *La France de l'intégration: sociologie de la nation en 1990* (Paris: Gallimard, 1991), 143.

36. Ibid., 139.

37. I am greatly indebted to Harry Markowicz and Carol Erting of Gallaudet University, and to Bernard Mottez, Centre National de la Recherche Scientifique, Paris, for their helpful criticisms of a first draft of this article. However, they should in no way be held responsible for the hazardous generalizations made here.

The Politics of Deafness

Deafness in French and American Society

HARRY MARKOWICZ, CAROL PADDEN,
AND CAROL ERTING

France and America will always be connected in a unique way: the language and culture of deaf people in America descended from France, and that history shall always remain with us—in the signs that our sign languages have in common and in the stories we tell about where deaf people came from and how their lives began. It makes sense to ask each other how our countries will make plans for the future of deaf children and deaf adults because our pasts are so intertwined.

As we make plans for the future, it is not enough to simply use each other as a model. We may both be Western countries with similar educational goals, but—and we want to emphasize an important point—there are significant historical, cultural, and political differences between the two countries. In order to learn from each other, indeed, cooperate with one another, we must be clear about where our differences lie.

To illustrate the point, we turn to the education of young deaf children. As we make plans for deaf children, it is not enough to study differences in educational "methods" or "approaches." It is not enough to say that in the United States we have Total Communication or that in France there is still oralism. Our differences also lie in

Harry Markowicz is associate professor, English department, Gallaudet University. **Carol Padden** is professor, department of communication, University of California at San Diego. **Carol Erting** is director, Culture and Communication Studies Program, Gallaudet University.

our political systems, in the structures of our societies, and even in our economic lives. For too long we have limited ourselves to talking about "education" or "rehabilitation"; we now need to realize that deaf people live in political, social, and economic worlds that affect their lives. We have to be clear-eyed about the real barriers and be ready to adapt to our own realities any idea or approach we borrow from each other.

Let us begin with a paradox. Many American professionals point to clear advances in the economic, social, and cultural integration of deaf adults in the United States. The economic lives of some deaf people have improved tremendously; there is now a strong professional, middle-class segment to the deaf adult population. Many of these deaf professionals not only participate in institutions that influence their lives, they are also directors, managers, and even presidents. Deaf adults can be found in a wide variety of professions, from medicine and science to education. Deaf high-school graduates can choose from among 150 different postsecondary educational programs. Each year more deaf people are awarded advanced degrees, including doctorates and law degrees.

A major factor in creating such educational possibilities has been the institutionalization of sign-language interpreting in the public sector. Federal laws now guarantee access to education and the judicial system, for example, through sign-language interpreters. Any university that receives federal funding must provide sign-language interpreters to deaf students or employees. Likewise, courts of law cannot put a deaf person on trial without sign-language interpreting services.

These laws have created an industry of sign-language interpreting; the largest professional organization of interpreters for deaf people in United States, the National Registry of Interpreters for the Deaf, now lists four thousand members.

Significant technological advances have accompanied these social and economic changes over the last ten or fifteen years—telecommunications devices for the deaf (TDDs) now exist not only within the deaf community but also in government offices and commercial establishments: nearly every major U.S. airline can be reached directly by TDD for reservations and information. Congress has TDDs that enable constituents to call their representatives. In 1990, Congress passed a major bill mandating a nationwide telephone relay between speaking and TDD-using people by 1993. These changes enable deaf people to communicate by telephone with virtually any person in the United States. Deaf people running businesses can use a relay service to communicate with their hearing customers, opening up new economic directions for the growing middle-class sector of the deaf community.

Not only have the public lives of deaf people in America changed, their private lives have changed as well. Each week, American television features over four hundred hours of closed-captioned or subtitled television programming. Captioning provides access to everyday popular culture, from football games to daytime soap operas and CNN PrimeNews. Deaf Americans are proud of these accomplishments for good reason—they were at the forefront of the political movements that brought them about.

And now to the paradox: in 1988, a commission appointed by Congress to investigate the education of deaf children reported that in spite of these major social and economic changes, deaf education is not what it should be. Reading levels of deaf students are still as dismally low as they were twenty or thirty years ago. Many professionals admit that too often residential schools for deaf children are unable to offer real educational challenges. Public Law 94-142, passed in 1975, was supposed to improve educational opportunities for deaf children by mainstreaming or integrating them into school programs for hearing students. Instead it has isolated many deaf children socially, culturally, and linguistically, offering no improvement, on balance, over residential schools.

How can we resolve this paradox? Why, with all the captions available on television programs, can we not raise a generation of deaf children who can read them?

One of the most important problems for us is the fact that while deaf people participate meaningfully in their social lives, they have not been permitted to have much influence on the education of deaf children. Schools for deaf children have been controlled by professionals who are not deaf and who, like school staff and administrators in general, are basically conservative and slow to change. The irony is that while we have deaf attorneys in the U.S. Department of Justice, there are graduate programs in deaf education that will openly tell deaf students they cannot teach preschool or elementary-aged deaf children because they are deaf. This pattern of discrimination is reflected in the distribution of deaf teachers in schools for deaf children: if deaf teachers are on the faculty, they are rarely teaching young children. Most often they are placed with adolescents and teenagers. The belief is that the early years of a deaf child's life are so important that they cannot be entrusted to deaf people—especially those who sign and do not speak.

Why are schools for deaf children so slow to change? In the United States, education is decentralized; educational policy is largely determined by local school districts, not by the federal government. One would think that the freedom of local school districts from a centralized policy would encourage them to be innovative. The opposite is true. Attempts at innovation are timid. An example is the movement toward bilingual education for deaf children, which has been talked about for fifteen to twenty years but is being attempted seriously in only three U.S. schools. The major trend is clearly toward mainstreaming, and deaf people still have very little influence on educational decisions.

It is important to understand that deaf people are fighting both the ideal of integration and the powerful economic incentive of mainstreaming. The federal government, through Public Law 94-142, gave more economic support to local school districts than to schools for deaf children. As a result, many school districts created programs for deaf children rather than sending them to a school for the deaf. Nevertheless, with time, it is becoming clear to many school districts that the cost of properly supporting deaf children is no longer less than sending them to schools for the deaf. As a result, a few school districts are rethinking their positions. In one school district in California, the local schools have reached an agreement with a school for the deaf to send more children there.

When we look to France, we see an entirely different educational system. France is highly centralized; all teachers must meet the same educational requirements, and the curriculum is uniform throughout the schools. But despite what appears to be less opportunity for experimentation, innovation has been occurring for more than ten years in deaf education. Martine Brusque, in an essay in this book, talks about deaf teachers without diplomas who teach classes of deaf children. Another contributor to this volume, Bernard Mottez, points out that within the Ministry of Education the employment of the deaf is still banned. However, classes taught entirely by deaf teachers can be found in several public schools. Although not yet implemented, a recent law passed within the framework of the Ministry of Solidarity allows parents to choose to have their children educated by the bilingual approach as an alternative to oral education. There is no such national recognition of bilingual education for deaf children in the United States.

Furthermore, and this is interesting, in France, the bilingual classes are concentrated at the preschool and primary levels. Most of the deaf teachers Brusque discusses teach at this level. This is in sharp contrast to the situation in the United States, where deaf people are discouraged from working with young deaf children. The French focus their entire bilingual education initiative on children of this age.

We need to discover what makes American education of the deaf so conservative and resistant to change. As we said earlier, it is not enough to attack teaching methods. We need to be clear about the political situations in both countries to be helpful to one another when considering change. We know improvements in the quality of deaf people's lives are possible—they have come about in our own generation. Why are we able to bring about closed-captioning in a relatively short time, but we struggle to make school districts accountable for what they do to deaf children who are mainstreamed? How can we bring about real change in the impoverished educational lives of deaf children?

We would like to repeat our call for cooperation—in light of our differences. As Americans, we want to learn more about the French initiatives in education and social policy. We also need to be honest about our accomplishments and our continuing struggles as we explain ourselves to the French people.

Thoughts about the American Situation

I. KING JORDAN

In the United States, we often speak of getting "back to our roots"—our beginnings—as a means of helping us understand who we are and what we are about. An example of that as it relates to the education of the deaf seems especially appropriate at this moment.

Picture, if you will, an evening in London, England. The year is 1815. The time is October. Young Thomas Hopkins Gallaudet has been in London since June 25, becoming increasingly frustrated in his unsuccessful attempts to gain access, on reasonable terms, to learning about systems for teaching deaf children. On this particular evening, he is going to a lecture and demonstration on teaching methods given by a team of visiting Frenchmen from the National Institution for Deaf-Mutes in Paris: the Abbé Sicard, director of the school, and two of his most accomplished pupils, Jean Massieu and Laurent Clerc.

Imagine now the excitement of Gallaudet, following this impressive program, when Sicard extends to him an unqualified invitation to come to Paris and study his teaching methods. These are the roots of the education of the deaf in the United States.

The roots are sunk deep in French soil, for not only did we get from France the knowledge base for our system of educating deaf students, we acquired an even more precious legacy in the person of Laurent Clerc, who returned to the United States with Gallaudet. Clerc was the ideal complement to Gallaudet: consummate teacher and role model nonpareil. The team of Gallaudet and Clerc moved

---

I. King Jordan is president of Gallaudet University.

---

swiftly to place education of the deaf on firm ground in our country. Their "firsts" for schools for the deaf in the United States are legion— first permanent school (American School for the Deaf in Hartford, Connecticut), the first deaf teacher of the deaf (Clerc himself), the first support for special education from a state government (the Connecticut legislature appropriated five thousand dollars to assist the new school), the first grant for special education from the federal government (Congress granted the new school twenty-three thousand acres of land, which was sold to provide money for buildings), and so on.

We can never erase the debt to France and her educators, nor do we wish to. It is a common history, a legacy we share and one that provides a bond of mutual goodwill.

During the 175 years since Gallaudet made his way to Paris, a number of other interesting collaborative activities have occurred between our countries. A rather recent one is of particular note, since it established the motivation for this colloquium. In 1989, Gallaudet University hosted the Deaf Way, an international festival and conference on the language, culture, and history of deaf people. The conference became a celebration of unparalleled dimension, surpassing our most ambitious dreams. Again, we are indebted to our friends from France both for their large delegation and for their significant contribution to the program. France had the largest number of presenters of any foreign country. The delegation included outstanding educators and leaders from the deaf community. We were delighted, as well, to have the outstanding delegation of students from the National School in Paris along with its director, Mr. Monod-Gayraud. Of particular significance was the marvelous film on the life of Abbe de l'Epée, developed by the French National Federation of the Deaf (FNSF) with support from the Fondation Franco-Américaine. The film was very well received by Deaf Way participants and was a delightful excursion into a chapter of history that we hold so dear. The major joint involvement of France and the United States was the culmination of a long history of collaborative events. I will leave to another day further reminiscing about our past associations and ask you to think with me now about present and future plans.

We must create an ambitious agenda for the 1990s and beyond. We should heed the advice of the American landscape architect Daniel Burnham when he said, "Make no little plans. They have no magic to stir men's blood." Our agenda should include a variety of exchanges—the sort of thing we have done from time to time in the past, but with greater scope as well as more definition of purpose— a sharing of ideas and culture, so that those bridges we have built together endure and become of greater use.

A number of exchange opportunities are rather obvious but bear repeating. We should, of course, have a vigorous exchange-scholar program. This is perhaps the easiest and most obvious way to interact. We have many common interests and much to learn from each other. My own university, for example, has a Chair of Deaf Studies, which is a one-year appointment for a visiting scholar from home or abroad. The chairholder can focus activities on a specific project or on several areas of teaching, research, and service. We have other opportunities for exchanges within our Research Institute as well as within our teaching departments. Gallaudet welcomes students from abroad. This extends to our Model High School, which has an active student exchange program. Our high-school and college-level art, drama, and cultural programs are also open to exchange opportunities. I use Gallaudet programs as examples because they are what I know best. Exchange opportunities abound in other programs in the United States. Let us not overlook joint and parallel research programs within the context of exchange. Such programs can mean working side by side even though there is an ocean between us.

Our country has been fortunate to provide leadership in offering higher education to our deaf citizens—not only at Gallaudet but in many other institutions. I am aware that we have provided France and other countries with assistance in planning and implementing higher-education programs for deaf persons. This is an area where we will continue to offer help based on strategies of value to deaf people. In all these matters we need to be concerned, first, with what is needed and what will have the greatest impact; then we will concern ourselves with the removal of constraints of time and resources in achieving our objectives.

It is appropriate to think for a few moments on some of the more general and global opportunities that await us. Many recent developments of a worldwide nature, as well as on a more local level, are very encouraging as they affect the disabled community. We see marked changes in public policy. New laws affirm the rights of deaf and other disabled people to communication access, a broader range of jobs, and public accommodations. Breakthroughs for disabled people come more slowly than the outward manifestations of equality that are embodied in laws and other public policy statements. True equality comes with changes in the hearts and minds of people. Here, too, we see significant evidence of improvement everywhere. New attitudes in the workplace are opening increasing numbers of professional opportunities. Deaf persons are entering career paths that would have been closed to them only a few years ago. Similarly, within the larger social milieu, deaf and other disabled persons are beginning to be accepted as equals.

The anthropologist Margaret Mead once said, "Never doubt that a small group of thoughtful, committed citizens can change the world. Indeed they are the only thing that can." Three years ago, a group of committed students changed Gallaudet University. It will never be the same as before the student protest—it now has a deaf president, a deaf provost, and a deaf majority on its governing board, including the chairman. It has achieved a greatly improved level of communication access and is fast assuming the character of a truly multilingual/multicultural community.

I am concerned, frankly, at what I see as a trend to separate the deaf community into groups. I see deaf people quarreling with deaf people. I see deaf people talking about hearing professionals who work with deaf people as if "hearing" is a dirty word. I am concerned. The deaf community is small already. We cannot divide into even smaller groups. Think about sign language. In the United States, people are grouped by how they sign. We have people grouped into sign ASL, PSE, SEE, SEE2, SSS, SSS2. . . . And we have the oralists standing in the wings, chuckling and thinking, "Divide and conquer."

I am concerned because I see these divisions as establishing the same shells we have worked so hard to come out of. I believe in deaf people, and I believe that by working together we can convince the world to believe in deaf people.

Today more than ever, barriers to deaf people are coming down.

Today more than ever before, we have *real* opportunities. Let us work together to capitalize on the opportunities and show the world that deaf people *can* do anything!

Everywhere we see evidence that great things can happen when people work together. Cooperation and collaboration are the keys. A small group of my compatriots joined colleagues from France, several years ago in LaBalme, to erect a plaque on the birthplace of Laurent Clerc, to honor this great Frenchman. In the spirit of his memory, I would challenge each of us to continue to "make no small plans" on behalf of deaf people.

What Is the Real Issue?

MICHEL EXERTIER

Let us suppose for one instant—but this is already a fatal error—that the deaf constitute a perfectly homogeneous category. It is the deaf who are generally felt to be at fault, who must improve, who create a problem. But in fact, what underlies this gulf between deaf adults and nondeaf adults? In France, it stems from the probably unconscious fact that the nondeaf Good Samaritans who take care of deaf children refuse to recognize that the deaf can grow up, stop being children, and become autonomous and independent; in short, that they can become equals. The nondeaf continue to see people who are deaf as children and pupils or at least as human beings needing "guidance." It perhaps has never occurred to nondeaf adults who "work for" the deaf that the deaf could manage without them. It is as if they see the deaf first as deaf and only secondarily as wage earners, parents, and so forth. In this way, nondeaf people perceive the deaf person always as an object under observation, to be rescued, equipped, given therapy, integrated, and the like.

Now, you cannot both take a therapeutic view of people and talk "to" them. What do the nondeaf do but talk *about* the deaf? When they think they are talking *to* the deaf, are they saying anything other than what the deaf should be, should do, should think? This kind of discourse creates a second exclusion, much worse than the original handicap. It is the discourse of the master to the slave, who must be persuaded of his or her inferiority and feel guilty about it.

And yet the deaf and the nondeaf need to talk to each other. We

Michel Exertier is administrator of the "Quality of Life" Department of the Economic and Social Council (Conseil Economique et Social).

need to learn from one another how to talk together. It is not just a language problem or a problem of differing logics or of forms of social power, be these all too real. It probably concerns unconscious images that the deaf and nondeaf throw at one another in the moments of psychodrama inherent in our interaction.

The point at issue is no longer to define what a "deaf" person or a "nondeaf" person is—which is what all the psychology and sociology textbooks go on about—but to perceive what "I" am for "you," what the deaf person and the nondeaf person are for one another, going beyond all the representations, stereotypes, and recriminations. What do we bring to each other that is new to the understanding of the relationship between the deaf and nondeaf? In any situation where the deaf and the nondeaf are associated, such as at school or at work, the issue is neither the deaf nor the nondeaf but the deaf *and* the nondeaf, taken together as opposite poles of the same problem.

The issue, then, is that we have to work on the intermediating situation. This requires work on oneself that is much more difficult than a simple adjustment or adaptation. We have to develop new representations, new languages, new systems of logic—in other words, create a genuine common culture.

This means that in the last resort all of us, deaf and nondeaf, are condemned to get along, for we stand or fall together. Indeed, this is an irreversible situation, for the deaf have spoken and are making themselves heard. Even if their frankness hurts the delicate ears of the nondeaf, they are not going to stop. The nondeaf are going to have to give the deaf their rightful place, to share with them without fear. We are condemned to working together, to agreeing on what we have to do and how to do it. What is our task as adults? To set an example? If so, an example of what? An example of dialogue, of cooperation between deaf and nondeaf people who are able to work and talk together. Deaf children (and those who are not deaf), seeing that this is possible, will invest in these forms of communication and internalize them, so that later, as adults, they will find their bearings.

It is the deaf and nondeaf adults, whether we coexist or live "divorced," who anticipate the type of relationship that today's deaf children, the citizens of tomorrow, will build between themselves and the nondeaf. That is why the nondeaf bear a major responsibility, and why their ability to acknowledge and welcome deaf adults and help them occupy *their* place governs the fate of deaf children.

The work of educating deaf children so they succeed in society will always be very difficult, never fully satisfying, and will always need to be taken up again and consolidated. The deaf adults who passionately throw themselves into such a task know this. Nondeaf institutions usually concede only minor roles to the deaf; the nondeaf authorities, at a loss to validate the contribution of the deaf, for whom the usual examinations have little meaning, try to justify their privileges. Here too we need to set an example, an example of innovation.

Were success easy, the deaf would have been the equals of the nondeaf ages ago, and there would be no handicaps and no deficiencies. The elements that constitute the essence of a human being—speech, language, and that unique and prior fact, the tongue—cannot be treated as instrumental, mechanical phenomena, amenable to easy repair. Rather than believe that the education of deaf children is easy, or blame ourselves for failures, we should arm ourselves with patience, faith, and intelligence, and never forget that the real issue is quite different from memorizing facts or acquiring linguistic skills. The real issue is mutual acceptance and mutual creativity, which implies also every kind of renunciation along the way.

Suppose We Listened to the Deaf

ARLETTE MOREL

Only the deaf are truly capable of understanding the needs of the deaf. Our Center for the Social Advancement of Deaf Adults is based on this premise. Headed by deaf managers and employing bilingual staff, this is the first center of its type in France. The creation of similar centers elsewhere in France is one of our aims. We also hope to change society's misconceptions and to transform society's attitude toward the deaf from negative to positive. However, this philosophy must first be harmonized with the wishes and desires of the deaf community, and this can be done only if the deaf assume the responsibility of directing centers similar to ours (assisted by bilingual secretaries and interpreters). They also need to work closely with associations of the deaf, including the French National Federation of the Deaf (FNSF), with the common goal of breaking down the barriers between the world of the deaf and the world of the hearing, while respecting their differences.

Despite their best intentions, people outside the deaf community —particularly those wishing to help the handicapped—should not undertake work in services such as ours. They tend to reinforce the negative attitudes of society toward deaf people. It is a popular fallacy that vocational training must be adapted to the needs of the deaf. Nothing could be further from the truth. Such measures merely perpetuate the negative view that deaf people have of themselves, an attitude dating back to birth, since 95 percent of deaf people are born to hearing families and are only too aware of their parents' distress. The

Arlette Morel is the executive director of the Center for the Social Advancement of Deaf Adults (Centre de Promotion Sociale des Adultes Sourds).

parents, totally unnerved by the diagnosis of their child's deafness, are overwhelmed by physicians and paramedics—whose approach is to repair, to compensate for the handicap—and they find themselves inexorably sucked into the "specialized" spiral.

People who are deaf lack communication in their early childhood. They are dragged from one type of reeducation center to another, feeling guilty because they fail to measure up to the standards imposed by their parents. Next they enter a school. The school invariably fails in its mission (to transmit knowledge), since it is in fact an establishment for the disabled, where the teaching staff and principals are almost entirely hearing. In addition, the vocational training covers only an extremely narrow range of manual trades. After vocational training, deaf people begin their work careers in a society that is made up of "normal" people. It is hardly surprising that after all this the deaf view themselves negatively. What is surprising is their excellent psychological health. Under conditions where "normal" people would have overflowed the psychiatric hospitals, deaf people get themselves organized and set up centers like ours.

Our center strives to provide access for the deaf community to the full range of professional associations via interpreters who are members of the National Association for Interpretation in Sign Language (ANPILS). Before any training is undertaken, however, it is often necessary to bring their knowledge of French up to par and to broaden their general knowledge, as well. Alas, the low level of teaching provided to the deaf tends to thwart our training efforts. It is generally recognized that most deaf people are illiterate and that the current methods of teaching school subjects in "specialized" establishments urgently need revision. For the 1990–91 school year, our center provided courses in French, English, and elementary computer science to approximately one hundred deaf adults. All courses were taught in sign language by deaf or bilingual hearing teachers (ten courses—eight deaf teachers, two hearing).

In today's society, people who lack specialized skills or who have obsolete qualifications are excluded from the business world. For the deaf, unemployment is no longer a question of the quantity of jobs but of quality. The skills sought on the labor market are increasingly specific, and as a result there are countless unemployed people and many unfilled jobs. If the deaf remain handicapped by lack of skill and knowledge, and if nothing is done to improve the training available to them, they will continue to swell the ranks of the unemployed.

Government authorities are generally uninterested in these matters, which they do not fully understand. We have no say in government policy, which is developed by persons outside of our community who consider us sick and in urgent need of care before being integrated into society. The authorities prefer to negotiate with "normal" representatives, a state of affairs that undermines our work and that derives from the fact that certain charitable organizations, particularly parents' associations, prefer to set up their own training centers rather than work with us toward a common goal. This is explained partly by the policy of state subsidization and partly by a fundamental inability to perceive deaf people as autonomous individuals with their own language and culture. Moreover, the people directing these associations do not speak our language at all or only poorly.

Any independent-minded deaf person, proud of the deaf language and culture, will strive to avoid these situations. It is too frequently forgotten that proper integration implies a respect for differences. The rejoinder will be that all deaf people who have attended the training centers are delighted with them. This deserves further analysis that goes beyond the scope of my paper.

Deaf people should be allowed to assume responsibility for themselves. While it is perfectly normal that parents' associations should look after their own children, it is humiliating, tactless, and hurtful that the associations should attempt to impose their "assistance" on us deaf adults. We are willing and able to work together, but each party must play an appropriate role in respecting our differences. To remedy the failures noted at every stage of the education and training of the deaf, it is vital that deaf teachers and deaf spokespersons, who have the approval of organizations like ours, be involved: with physicians and parents during early childhood; in centers and hospitals that receive multihandicapped deaf people; in schools; in training centers for deaf adults (and during courses with the hearing); in all organizations responsible for supporting training activities; and with government representatives whenever they discuss laws and other matters affecting the deaf.

Advocacy and Agendas in the United States

ROSLYN ROSEN

The National Association of the Deaf (NAD) is the oldest advocacy organization of, for, and by deaf people in the United States and possibly in the world. It was established in 1880, the same year that the International Congress on Education of the Deaf in Milan, Italy, passed its now infamous resolution against the use of sign language. Since its inception, NAD has served as a national leader and crusader for the rights of deaf people and global deaf awareness. Its accomplishments have included lobbying for basic rights and entitlements: to drive vehicles, to marry other deaf people, to adopt children, to have insurance, and to obtain jobs and promotions. Advocacy strategies have ranged from publishing factual, research-based articles and books, lectures, and training sessions, to lobbying, litigating, and coalition building. Deaf people themselves determine the agenda at NAD conventions and become involved in the implementation of strategies.

The last three decades have marked significant progress. During the 1960s, with the advent of the TDD/modem (teletypewriter device for phone dialogue between deaf and nondeaf people), deaf people could finally participate in distance communications, but they still needed to wait another twenty-five years before relay service became a reality in some states. The 1960s also witnessed the birth of the Registry of Interpreters for the Deaf, which elevated interpreting into

Roslyn Rosen is currently vice-president for academic affairs at Gallaudet University and is a former president of the National Association of the Deaf.

a profession requiring training, certification, and a code of ethics and standards. However, appropriateness, quality, and consumer rights remain critical issues today. The 1960s was also the decade of civil rights for minorities and women, as well as consumer rights—movements that, although not directly applicable to deaf people, became building blocks for future legislative action and new mind-sets.

The 1970s brought us closed-captioned television programs, which gave deaf people their first opportunity to receive news, information, and entertainment at the same time as their hearing family members, neighbors, and peers. This was also the decade when sign language came out of the closet and went public, as did the philosophy of Total Communication, which affirmed the deaf child's right to understand, to be understood, and to participate in the dynamics of a situation, whether at home, in school, or on the playground, and with whatever the methodologies may work—whether signed or oral or combinations thereof. This new philosophy opened many homes and classroom doors to the use of natural, visual, manual communication—American Sign Language (ASL)—and also to the proliferation of manual communication systems. In 1975, the enactment of U.S. Public Law 94-142, now known as the Individuals with Disabilities Education Act (IDEA), introduced the "least restrictive environment" concept, often misinterpreted as a mandate for each local school district to include, in mainstream fashion, all eligible students with disabilities in regular public schools. A year later, regulations and amendments to the Vocational Rehabilitation Act of 1973 prohibited discrimination, on the basis of disability, in education, employment, and services.

The 1960s and '70s set the stage for a sense of human rights, dignity, and empowerment for deaf people. They became more involved in determining their own lives and programs for their own people. Service agencies with the "of, for, and by deaf people" philosophy emerged in this era to lead local efforts at self-determination and self-help and to collaborate, in network fashion, with state associations of the deaf and other organizations.

The emergence of deaf rights does not mean that, by magic, equality and human rights became part and parcel of the lives of all deaf Americans. There remain many barriers, the foremost being attitudinal. Example: doctors still give parents the impression that deafness is a tragedy and that it might be fixed with a cochlear implant, or at least that deafness might be made to go away by practicing hearing and speaking like normal folks. Example: some people equate speech with intelligence and therefore a better quality of life. Example: some believe that phonetics must be learned before one can master language and literacy. Example: some believe that signs will hurt speech and that ASL will hurt mastery of English. Example: some believe that the goal in life should be to blend in with society (and the woodwork) as much as possible. And that going to public schools is a mark of normalcy, whereas going to special schools indicates deviation and inferiority. Example: some cannot believe that hearing is actually not essential for 99 percent of jobs. Example: deaf persons or professionals are not generally encouraged to work with deaf toddlers or their families or in mainstream schools. Example: some did not believe that a deaf person could be president of Gallaudet University. And saddest of all: these examples are not limited to nondeaf people. Deaf people, victims of the years of oppression from the cradle onward, become perpetuators of their own suppression and deaf-defeatism.

Little did the board of trustees of Gallaudet University dream that they would change the course of history and redefine human rights when they initially chose a nondeaf president in 1988! Gallaudet became the center of the universe for that one week as the world watched, became engulfed by the drama, and became active supporters of the deaf community in its quest for self-governance and validation. Everyone, deaf and nondeaf, became believers in the can-do mind-set. The cause was supported by deaf people, hearing Gallaudet employees, families with deaf members, people with disabilities, people of color, the media, and Congress! Unity brought power. The result, a forever-altered perception of deafness and people with disabilities, helped launch passage of the Americans with Disabilities Act of 1990, a sweeping civil rights act that encompasses all life functions in the public and private sectors.

The trickle-down effect for the average American is a new, more positive image that is closer to reality. First, as Gallaudet's president, I. King Jordan, has declared, "Deaf people can do anything but hear!"

Second, positive deaf role models have emerged to serve as beacons of light and hope for thousands of people, both deaf and nondeaf. Young deaf children have been inspired to emulate successful deaf people in all walks of life. Parents have been exposed to deaf role models, often for the first time. Professionals and employees have become interested in supporting and empowering deaf people. That one week in the media spotlight generated a synergy of ripple effects.

An optimist might conclude that NAD, having helped achieve these goals, should put itself out of business for lack of a mission. However, it is now back to reality and the need to effect lasting change in the way deaf people are educated and served. This brings us to today's deaf people and the national agenda for NAD and for us all. The picture is not rosy.

Our major concern is to shift paradigms and alter people's mindsets. This means changing permanently from old to new perceptions and attitudes.

First, we must change from *paternalism* to *partnership*, from doing things *for* or *to* deaf people to doing things *with* or *under* deaf people. Once, at a major airport that advertised full accessibility for passengers with disabilities, I checked its brochure describing services, specifically the part regarding deaf travelers, and I received the instruction, "Deaf passengers should go to the nearest red telephone and call for a TDD." Obviously, the well-meaning but ill-advised administrators who wrote the brochure acted without the involvement of deaf people and therefore produced advice that is nonsense. As the saying goes, "You must walk a mile in another person's shoes before you can understand what it means to be that person." Only deaf people understand what it means to be deaf. They must lead, and nondeaf persons need to become supporters and partners for mutually desirable goals.

Second, we must change from *pathological* to *humanistic* approaches. This means changing from the medical view of deafness, as a deviation to be fixed, to the humanistic view of deafness. It is dandy to be deaf! This is one reason why NAD, along with the World Federation of the Deaf, opposes cochlear implants for children too young to make their own decisions. Parents who do not receive false "hopes" can move more easily past grieving and the denial of deafness to the business of living and loving.

Third, we must move from perceiving society as *homogenized* to recognizing that it is *culturally diverse*. Instead of retaining a "one size fits all" mentality or trying to emulate the WASP mold, we must cherish human multiplicity, including variations in ethnicities, races, genders, religions, and many other human differences, including hearing and not hearing.

Fourth, we must turn from *monolingualism* to *bilingualism* and even *trilingualism*. In many countries, residents are encouraged to know at least two languages, but in the United States, English reigns supreme. However, there is an increasing awareness and acceptance of the legitimacy of native or natural languages in the United States. For deaf people, bilingualism means American Sign Language and English. Moreover, the true language of signs is one that conforms to visual and linguistic principles appropriate for a three-dimensional language, which facilitates natural and comfortable communication for visually dependent persons. Trilingualism occurs among deaf people born to non-English-speaking families. Academic programs in Deaf Studies must also be available.

Fifth, we must move beyond *simple access* to *quality of access*. Access is the law, but quality remains elusive. Access of poor quality is not access! Quality standards for educational professionals and educational programs must be developed by and with deaf consumers. Interpreters need to meet standards determined by deaf consumers. Communications and safety-light systems need to be designed in collaboration with deaf people to ensure appropriateness. Programs must meet standards that surpass minimal expectations and enable more than marginal participation. If one cannot access or benefit from services or programs, one might as well stay home.

Sixth is the need to move from *dependence* to *independence*. Ninety percent of deaf children are born to hearing families. The 10 percent born to deaf families often become models of excellence in education, communications, leadership, and society in general. The challenge, then, is to identify the factors producing positive self-esteem, educational excellence, affective well-being, and environmental enhancers

in all-deaf families and to transplant them into nondeaf families with
deaf children. Several factors come readily to mind. In addition to
more immediate acceptance of deafness, they include high expectations, full and visual communications, and a barrier-free home where
deaf children have full information and a greater degree of independence. All-deaf homes are more likely to have the full array of technological aids, such as TDDs, TV decoders, flashing or vibrating alarm
clocks, and flashing-light signals for doorbells and phones. Deaf children also participate in discussions during family meals and find that
their opinions are valued.

Seventh is the vital switch from the *can't* mind-set to the *can-do*
attitude. Deaf people can do anything. They can be doctors, auto-
mobile mechanics, computer programmers, dentists, engineers, construction supervisors, plumbers, administrators, lawyers, and so on.

These general principles of change define the seven major social
reforms that NAD and the deaf community seek:

1. *Early identification* of deafness and appropriate intervention
   measures, including early involvement of signing deaf professionals (as role models) with families with deaf infants. Information for parents must be from the deaf viewpoint and must
   include the obvious fact that the deaf child will always be visually oriented.
2. *Full communication access and quality,* as defined by the deaf
   consumer. Professionals harm instead of help when they give
   parents material about all possible communication and educational options without supporting information on each and
   without the involvement of deaf adults. Parents will naturally
   want their child to be as much like themselves as possible and
   will probably choose oralism; only after struggling with that
   will they finally accept that their child is *deaf.* We believe in telling parents to give their child both sign language and speech—
   in short, everything. Research has shown that sign language
   does not harm oral skills. To the contrary, deaf children of deaf
   parents often demonstrate superior skills in both the native language of signs and the spoken language.

   In public settings—schools, workplaces, the community—

the deaf persons involved in meetings or programs must receive communication support services of a quality that meets standards set by the consumers themselves. They are the only true judges of what is adequate and what is not.

3. *A Bill of Educational Rights,* including the right to be in a fully enabling environment. In line with the national goals of regular education, deaf children should likewise be able to enter school ready to learn and to attain skills to graduate with their grade level. This is true for deaf children of deaf parents! Hearing children expect to go to a school where they can understand and be understood by the other children and by the adults. To extend this right to deaf children means limiting options to those schools that can provide a fully enabling environment with peers and adults who can communicate comfortably and fluently. This is best done in magnet schools and in schools that have both deaf and nondeaf teachers and administrators fluent in communicating with deaf people.

4. *Bilingualism and biculturalism* as the birthright of each deaf child. Families need to understand that the visual dependency of their child mandates visually clear communication and an understanding of the child's essence and identity. Rather than be doomed to a twilight world without a solid language, culture, or identity, the child is empowered by knowing both American Sign Language and English, being part of both the deaf and nondeaf cultures.

5. *Employment* as an essential life function contributing to self-esteem. Deaf people must not only become gainfully employed but must also choose vocations based on their interests and abilities. By law, jobs may be altered in order to accommodate individuals with disabilities. Therefore, a broad career education is essential not only for deaf students but also for career counselors, families, and employers, who will be able to counsel students better.

6. *Community life* for deaf people that is the same as for nondeaf people. Community services and features—libraries, museums, theaters, welfare and health services, transportation, housing—need to be accessible and appropriate for deaf people. Deaf

people must be informed and involved in determining the standards for accessibility and quality.

7. *Empowerment,* meaning full involvement and leadership for deaf people. For example, if a school, whether special or mainstreamed, has a significant number of deaf students, does its board include deaf adults representing the interests of the deaf students? If a business or community is planning a new program, are deaf leaders part of the planning team? In a program basically for deaf people, do deaf people constitute a majority of the planning team or board, or are they tokens? If a new policy or law is being considered, are deaf people consulted? The empowerment of deaf people also means the empowerment of parents and professionals who feel successful and positive in their roles as partner-advocates.

In the United States, the recognition of the right to be different and to assemble with one's kind has led to the establishment of many different groups within the deaf community. The deaf community itself has a wide variety of organizations to choose from, organizations that address interests ranging from sports to religion, as well as consumer organizations related to ethnicities, races, and degree and age of onset of deafness: Black Deaf Advocates, National Association of Deaf Hispanics, Self-Help for the Hard of Hearing, Association of Late-Deafened Americans, Oral Deaf Adults Section of the AGB, and the newly formed Cochlear Implant Club International.

In addition to this network are the organizations of the service providers: Telecommunications for the Deaf, Inc. (TDI), the Conference of Educational Administrators Serving the Deaf, the Conference of American Instructors of the Deaf, the American Deafness and Rehabilitation Association, the Registry of Interpreters for the Deaf, and a family-based organization supported by NAD, the American Society for Deaf Children. NAD has provided assistance to the Coalition of Organizational Representatives (COR), which is an informal body of representatives of these and related organizations who meet once monthly to share information, discuss legislative issues, and support mutual goals.

NAD is also starting up a coalition of affiliates, composed of organizations that are of, for, and by deaf people, in order to gain a broader base of consumer representation. Enacted at the 1990 NAD convention, the effort will require time before it becomes fully operational as a consumer-driven entity seeking social and political action. One illustration of why this organization is needed comes from a recent decision by COR to support minimal requirements for the telecommunications section of the new Americans with Disabilities Act. For example, COR considered acceptable a 35-word-per-minute typing speed for telephone relay operators, whereas NAD, in its own comments to the federal government, insisted on at least 60 words per minute. The outcome was adoption of a final standard of 60 words per minute within two years, a higher standard that will benefit both deaf and hearing consumers. We, the deaf people of America, believe that deaf consumers should be in the forefront of political changes and standards that affect deaf people. We need and welcome nondeaf partners and nondeaf allies, but it is essential that services by, for, and of deaf people be defined by, for, and of deaf people. To do otherwise is a travesty of human rights and a mockery of the right to self-determination inherent in every human being.

Where do we go from here? Join with us, walk beside us, and be our partners toward a more progressive future where people are accepted *for* themselves rather than *in spite of* themselves.

References

Gannon, J. *Deaf Heritage: A Narrative History of Deaf America.* Silver Spring, Md.: National Association of the Deaf, 1981.

Gannon, J. *The Week the World Heard Gallaudet.* Washington, D.C.: Gallaudet Press, 1988.

Garretson, M., ed. "Communication Issues among Deaf People, a Deaf American Monograph." *The Deaf American* 40 (1990).

Lane, Harlan. "Cochlear Implants for Deaf Children: A NAD Position Paper." *The NAD Broadcaster* (March 1991).

Rosen, R., ed., *Life and Work in the 21st Century: The Deaf Person of Tomorrow.* Silver Spring, Md.: National Association of the Deaf, 1986.

Rosen, R. "Deafness: A Social Perspective." In *Deafness in Perspective,* D. Luterman. San Diego: College-Hill Press, 1986.

Public and Private Initiatives

ROSE-MARIE RAYNAUD

In a document referring to urban access for the disabled, a deaf member of our association wrote the following introduction: "The problem of integration is as old as the hills and will of course always be with us. We shall only succeed in approaching it as society evolves, matures, and takes full account of the deep-rooted meaning of *solidarity* in its operations."

Since every disabled person is, by definition, dependent, the dream of autonomy is no more than a dream. If we can only begin to approach it through appropriate education and technical progress, the dream still leaves all concerned with the reality of a handicap, induced by attitudes to an impairment, which calls for mutual assistance. One cannot continue to deny the interactive nature of a relationship without betraying oneself. Thus, for example, we are "dumb" when faced with the deaf, "crippled" with the blind, "blind" with the crippled, stupid with people with Down syndrome, and so on. What really counts is not the technical success of an integration policy but the way the policy is implemented, the underlying attitudes, the breadth of its goals, and, to put it simply, the functioning of "true" democracy.

Accurate information must be the underlying basis for deaf action. The deaf must themselves assume responsibility for disseminating information on their problems: what deafness really means and how to convey the message to the hearing. The hearing need to know that a deaf person has the same intellectual, vocational, and artistic abilities

Rose-Marie Raynaud is president of the French National Federation of the Deaf (Fédération Nationale des Sourds de France).

as they do. They need to know how to address the deaf and how to converse with them.

The French National Federation of the Deaf (FNSF) is one among several organizations that are represented by the National Union for the Social Integration of the Hearing-Impaired (UNISDA), an association created as an umbrella for the diverse needs and viewpoints of the deaf and hearing impaired in France. Each organization represented by UNISDA has its own focus and character. My organization, the FNSF, consists mainly of persons born deaf. They seek integration at the highest possible level in hearing society, yet they also consider themselves part of the deaf community, where they employ French Sign Language (LSF).

Other organizations have different perspectives. The Coordination Bureau of Associations of the Late-Deafened and Hearing Impaired (BUCODES) represents the late-deafened and hearing impaired, a statistically large group in France whose members are nevertheless often isolated and forgotten. People in this category can speak French perfectly but often have difficulty in understanding speech by the hearing, despite the use of lipreading. The National Association of Parents of Hearing-Impaired Children (ANPEDA) consists of parents seeking to improve education for children and teenagers in both specialized and mainstream programs. They stress the irreplaceable role of the family in education. The Central Society for Education and Assistance to Deaf Mutes in France, established in the nineteenth century, assists all persons concerned in any way with deafness. The Liaison and Action Committee of Parents of Children and Adults Suffering from Multiple Disabilities (CLAPEAHA) deals with the problems of the multi-disabled deaf.

Member organizations of UNISDA offer a wide array of services, including courses for the parents of hearing-impaired children; lipreading courses for late-deafened adults; congresses, symposia, and sporting events; and the promotion of access to information and culture through Minitels (visually accessible telephones) and the subtitling of films—to mention just a few. My own organization, the FNSF, has persuaded the Postgraduate School of Interpreters and Translators (ESIT) in Paris to organize two three-week seminars for sign-language interpreters. These seminars, designed to test teaching methods to be implemented in the technical-sciences master's degree curriculum, have been successful. The faculty includes academics, professional conference interpreters, and deaf persons.

The FNSF has also established many contacts with legislators interested in the problems of deafness. During a recent budget debate in the National Assembly, Laurent Fabius and members of the Socialist Group successfully amended Article 19 to require "freedom of choice between bilingual communication—sign language and French—and oral communication" in the education of the young deaf. A decree by the Conseil d'Etat will define how this freedom is to be exercised and the institutional arrangements needed to ensure that choice really exists. The National Assembly also adopted the general principle that the deaf have a right to bilingual communication (sign language and French) and oral communication. The deaf child thus appears to have a guaranteed right of choice. In a nutshell, French Sign Language (LSF) has been officially recognized.

In the area of public initiatives, television is the primary medium for informing the hearing about the deaf and for enabling them to achieve better integration into the hearing world. The efforts made to date are, unfortunately, quite inadequate. The deaf person's image of television resembles that of a toy handed to a child as a pacifier. The problem is, the deaf are not children but full-fledged citizens who have the same rights (in theory) and the same responsibilities as everyone else: they pay taxes and the television license. A deaf person buys a television set because he or she has the same knowledge (however vague, alas!) as anyone about the techniques and the resources that this modern marvel would seem to offer: programs subtitled or interpreted in sign language. It is enough to make the mouth water!

But the reality is entirely different. It begins at our level. We are an association officially recognized as being "in the public interest." The authorities have emphasized "the obligation" for television channels to "gradually adapt their TV programs to the difficulties of the deaf and hearing-impaired, after consulting the representatives of the latter as to the choice of programs to be made accessible to their members." For the television consumer, the following must be noted. Newscasts for the deaf and hearing impaired are broadcast on Saturdays, just before 11 a.m., too late for people who have to leave early for work. They have been whittled down from thirty minutes to only twenty, so one needs to be quick on the uptake. They offer translation in sign language or, more frequently, in signed French, but the translation is hard to follow; and the newscasters speak so fast that it is hard to lip-read. There is a tendency to cover important events without translation. Too bad the events don't convert the deaf into hearing!

There are other points worth noting. Children have no programs directed at them, nor do teenagers. What remains to these hearing-impaired persons if they have no television? Broadcasts of Sunday mass often suffer because the camera operators tend to focus on the cathedral vaults or the congregation instead of the cleric and the interpreter. Another bane is the programming of subtitled foreign films in the original-language version too late at night to serve the early riser who must leave for work or school the next morning. In any event, such films are few, and their often complex vocabulary often makes it hard to read the rapidly moving subtitles. The real solution to problems like this is the use of a special decoder. The decoder changes the daily life of the deaf user and is clearly the best solution. It is gaining favor among the young, since its teletext newscasts provide coverage twenty-four hours a day, and other services provide a wide array of information about laws, social services, recreation, culture, and the like.

What can I say by way of conclusion? If I take an issue of the French-American Foundation's newsletter, *Passport,* I find an article entitled "France/USA—Reluctant Fascination." I would rather phrase it "France/USA—Mutual Fascination." We French are fascinated by what is being done for the deaf in the United States.

First of all, Gallaudet University is a token of the brilliant success of the American deaf, who have access to a variety of professions. To cap it all, the university is headed by a deaf person.

France is proud to have been involved in the birth of the university, for it was Thomas Gallaudet, together with one of our citizens, Laurent Clerc, a deaf person and a former graduate and teacher at the National School for the Deaf in Paris, who established the basis for this institution.

After observing what has been achieved in the United States in the fields of television and the telephone, our federation has contacted ministries and other authorities to enable the French deaf to benefit from similar advantages through subtitled television programs and the Minitel dialogue for telephones. In the field of education, for some years now the French deaf have gained access to universities and a number of professions previously closed to them. We sincerely hope that there will more exchanges and other contacts between the deaf people of France and the deaf people of the United States.

Aspects of a French-American Comparison

BERNARD MOTTEZ

A Few Historical Reminders

In 1965, a new protagonist broke onto the deafness scene. A group of angry parents established the National Association of Parents of Hearing-Impaired Children (ANPEDA). They rejected their children's isolation, from earliest life, in specialized residential institutions. They repudiated an educational system that lacked any ambition other than relegating their children to the manual trades. Hostile to all forms of segregation, they questioned every aspect of age-old routines, changed the rules of the game, and established new alliances. Fiercely supporting the oral method, their principal targets being specialized schools and traditional teachers, they placed their hopes in physicians and paramedical support staff. They sought their children's integration into ordinary classes.

At ANPEDA's twenty-fifth anniversary in 1990, its founders rightly claimed to have made a lasting impression. They succeeded. Today they possess human, material, and strategic assets incomparably greater than those of the French National Federation of the Deaf (FNSF). Their influence and enterprising spirit extend well beyond the schools. Their initial work focused on the introduction of early screening programs, early use of hearing aids, and preschool edu-

Bernard Mottez is director of research at the National Center for Scientific Research (Centre National de la Recherche Scientifique), Center for the Study of Social Movements (Centre d'Etude des Mouvements Sociaux).

cation, and has expanded to cover a far broader scope, including day-care hospitals, programs and facilities for deaf students, and integration into the professions.

The United States has no comparable organization, no parents' lobby. You cannot understand the situation in France if you ignore ANPEDA.

In 1973, another uniquely French organization, the National Union for the Social Integration of the Hearing-Impaired (UNISDA), was created on the principle that union is strength. Associations of the deaf, the deafened, and of parents who had assisted in the planning of the Congress of the World Federation of the Deaf (Paris, 1971) formed UNISDA as a broad-based organization for representing what are now termed consumers or users. Professionals specializing in the deaf and deafness or their associations and unions were therefore excluded from the new body. UNISDA has helped advance the platform of the FNSF, though some observers believe it has maintained too lofty a position. Others believe that since "union" implies that only those points on which all members agree will be adopted, the organization has tended to avoid certain important issues, particularly in the area of sign language.

Contacts between the French and Americans were occasional and loosely organized until 1975, the year of the Congress of the World Federation of the Deaf, in Washington, D.C. In the summer of 1991, Bernard Truffaut, while recounting our common history at a symposium on the history of the deaf, stressed one major point: this new exchange differed from all previous ones inasmuch as summer meetings were being replaced by contact at the grassroots level. Several Americans who had spent years living in France threw open the gates of the United States and shared their feelings with us, freely imparting their knowledge and know-how. They were typical of the United States in the 1970s, the land of civil rights, where minorities fought for the right to live openly as they really are and wish to be, not as others want them to be. This was an era of growing cultural assertiveness on the part of African Americans, a time of both women's liberation and gay liberation. This was the awakening of ethnic awareness.

The awakening of the deaf took place along similar lines. The refrain was as follows: we are not diseased and in need of care and cure, but rather a linguistic minority who want acceptance as such and public recognition of our language. This message had a good chance of being accepted in France, since there too the 1970s was a decade of identity movements—the right to be different. Then it was also recalled that when the French government banned deaf teachers and sign language from the classroom in 1880, it also began an offensive in the public schools against minority languages.

Not all deaf persons perceive and claim their social integration in this way. Some do not feel they belong to the deaf world or make it a point of honor never to use sign language. The vast majority of those who consider themselves part of the deaf world follow the traditional wisdom of the powerless: keep hidden. Let us keep to ourselves on the fringe of society.

The movements of the 1970s, however, sent a message to the militant deaf, whose numbers were increasing year by year. They were beginning to leave their construction sites, workshops, and offices to teach their language to the hearing and to involve themselves in the teaching of deaf children. In general, they operated within the framework of associations, created usually in cooperation with hearing parents and professionals who shared their points of view. The most militant of all was an association known as Two Languages for One Education (2 LPE). Like the Academy of French Sign Language (ALSF), it was modeled after the Gallaudet University summer courses and referred specifically to their teachings. The association's tenets included adoption of the "Deaf Pride" philosophy of Barbara Kannapell and the findings of William Stokoe's linguistics research laboratory at Gallaudet University, which were critical of Total Communication and advocated bilingualism. Members of the association tried to convey both their language and their convictions to all involved in deafness issues. Their militant approach, similar to that of ANPEDA's pioneers, rested on the same dual refusal: not to remain marginalized and not to accept the mediocre educational system designed for the deaf. But the two movements reached diametrically opposed diagnoses and solutions. While ANPEDA advocated speech at all cost and in all cases, the militants lobbied for sign language, bilingualism, and interpreters in public places. The militants preferred the return of deaf professionals, the true specialists in deafness, over the proliferation of multiple specialists and the "miraculous" educational gadgets that seemed to be reinvented every decade.

All professionals and specialists have had to take note of these historical developments, which are mutually contradictory. Policymakers and administrators have also had to address these issues and facts when trying to create new rules of the game.

Today

Identity movements are felt to be threatening today. Only their errors and excesses tend to be remembered. The *right to be different* is no longer popular in France and is often regarded as a fad or a mistake. Instead we brandish *equality,* a value inherited from the French Revolution. Recently a major report on the integration of immigrants offered an occasion to forcibly reassert integration French-style. Contrary to the Anglo-American approach, which rests on recognizing communities, the French option recognizes only individuals. The dormant Jacobin, or centralist, in every French person tends to consider the recognition of any other community or particular culture as an affront to equality and a threat to individual freedom. Any policy that caters to specific groups or communities is perceived as expressing a form of racism and segregation, with all the attendant risks.

This was undoubtedly one of the deeply rooted instincts that led to the rejection of the idea of a deaf community, a deaf culture, a deaf language—and Gallaudet University—particularly by those most attached to the principles of *laïcité,* which stress adherence to a single national culture and language. The true integration of the deaf means their integration not only into hearing schools, as in English-speaking countries, but also into the national educational system, which holds closely to the principle of *laïcité* and refuses to deal with religious, cultural, or ethnic diversity. The education of the deaf in France was regarded as tantamount to charity work and still depends heavily on ministries other than the Ministry of Education.

Official speechifying during the past fifteen years on the theme of a "multicultural" France has produced few results, at least as far as minority languages are concerned. None of the results compares with the bilingual projects in American schools. It should be stressed, however, that American projects were not designed to develop minority languages and cultures. They tried to introduce Spanish speakers and young Native Americans to the English language and American culture. This is precisely the opposite of the aims of certain French bilingual classes that use regional languages. In these programs, militants attempt to revive declining languages that are often nearly forgotten by the parents who send their French-speaking children to the classes.

Sign language is not on the decline. It is in full swing all over the world. An increasing number of the deaf and even the hearing speak it. Far from creating the ghettos some critics predicted and which the French constantly brandish as a threat, the recognition of sign language together with the development of interpretation have been the strongest contributors to the emergence of the American deaf from their ghetto. Sign language is a fact of life in the United States, and no one questions it. We in France are far from having reached that stage.

In certain fields, however, we French have actually taken things a step further than the Americans because we learned the lessons of the American experience. After the Deaf Way conference, in July 1989, some French deaf feared that English had made serious inroads into ASL, so much so that ASL was becoming merely a kind of signed English. I believe that in France a tendency to purism is linked to the marginal, precarious status of French Sign Language and of deaf professionals. There is still no public teaching of French Sign Language. Most of the new generation of hearing teachers are unable to sign. As for deaf professionals, they are numerous only because of a decade of daring efforts supported by intelligent, courageous administrators. Order has now returned, however; the employment of the deaf in the Ministry of Education is still banned. Employment of the deaf under the umbrella of another agency, the Ministry of Solidarity, is now sanctioned but stringently regulated. We are coming to the end of an epoch.

Interpreting for the Deaf and Hearing

Interpreting for Deaf and Hearing People in the United States

BILL MOODY

The professional interpreter in American Sign Language and English is a relatively new phenomenon: our Registry of Interpreters for the Deaf, RID, celebrated its twenty-fifth anniversary in 1991. Because we are young and still searching for our professional identity, I will dwell here on the history of our organization and our evolving views of what constitutes a professional interpreter. Lou Fant's book *Silver Threads,* published in 1991 by the RID, served in part as a basis for this paper.

Our Beginnings

The RID was established in 1964 during a national workshop in Indiana entitled "Interpreting for the Deaf." The workshop was convened to address the problem of the shortage of sign-language interpreters. The participants agreed that an organization was needed to maintain a list, or registry, of qualified interpreters and to assess their competency. Of seventy-three participants at the workshop, more than half were educators working in deaf schools; only three participants called themselves interpreters.

In fact, interpreters at that time either grew up signing with their deaf parents or had daily contact with deaf people working in schools for the deaf. Sign-language interpreters, generally with close ties to

Bill Moody is a sign-language interpreter and author.

the deaf community but with no professional training, volunteered their services out of a sense of duty or to promote the general welfare of the deaf. Interpreting was a sideline activity, not a profession, and to be paid for interpreting was rare indeed. Interpreters were generally very fluent in ASL though none had any formal training as interpreters: most had deaf parents and had learned ASL as their first language.

The interpreters and deaf people at this first organizational meeting became charter members of our new association, and a board of five officers, one of whom was deaf, was established to run the RID. Other interpreters and deaf people could join on the recommendation of two members. The new association aimed to promote the recruitment and training of more interpreters, and to develop a code of ethics.

In 1967, the RID secured a federal grant to establish a home office in the building of the National Association of the Deaf (NAD) in Washington, D.C. The first executive director, Al Pimentel, was himself deaf. After five years at the NAD, the RID moved to Gallaudet University for a short time before establishing its own home office.

Beginning in 1970, the RID held biennial conventions where its members could meet and keep up with the changes in the profession. Local RID chapters proliferated around the country.

During the 1970s, linguistic research on ASL began to be published widely, and RID members increasingly saw ASL as a language in its own right and interpreting as a professional occupation. There was much talk of Deaf Culture and of ASL having a spatial grammar distinct from that of the English language.

The RID code of ethics sought to ensure the impartiality and confidentiality of interpreters, as well as discretion in dress and professional behavior. The professional interpreter was expected to recognize his or her own limits in accepting assignments, and to seek the assistance of other interpreters when necessary (including calling on a qualified deaf person as a "relay" interpreter when the communication was difficult or delicate). It has now been more than two decades since the development of this original code of ethics, and a major revision is overdue. We may now have enough experience to begin writing an ethics casebook containing specific hypothetical situations with recommended ethical responses that could serve as useful guidelines for interpreters in the field.

Recruiting New Interpreters

By 1970, the market for interpreting services was already booming. Deaf students in increasing numbers were demanding their right to attend hearing universities around the country, accompanied by interpreters. Social service agencies were beginning to call on interpreters to serve deaf clients. With the creation of more and more jobs for full-time interpreters, it became obvious that new interpreters would have to be recruited.

Because there were not enough fluent hearing signers interested in becoming interpreters, any new candidates for these jobs first had to *learn* sign language. Classes sprang up everywhere: in churches, homes, and social service agencies (it was only in the 1980s that sign language was taught with established curricula in the universities). Sign-language teachers across the country generally had no training in second-language learning and invented their lesson plans as they went along. Unfortunately, the teaching of sign language was generally limited to classes in sign vocabulary building. Though linguists had begun their research into ASL's grammar, their work rarely filtered down to sign-language teachers in the field. As a result, new interpreter "recruits," having learned Sign as a second language in classes rather than growing up in the deaf community, did not communicate as naturally in ASL as did the older interpreters. Most of these new "interpreters" produced more a version of Signed English than ASL. Some of them had trouble understanding deaf people at all.

Even when the rare ASL student really *did* become fluent in ASL, he or she still lacked the necessary second step: *interpreter* training. The first pilot training programs were not even established until 1973, when a federal grant funded six pilot interpreter-training programs around the country (in 1978, the number doubled to twelve programs). Instructors in these pilot programs tried their best to train interpreters with very little research to help in planning their curricula. Interpreter trainers, with much interpreting experience in the field but little or no training themselves, developed curricula as they went along. Most trainers tried to keep up with linguistic research in ASL as it was published. But without recognized standards and accreditation procedures, the results of interpreter training programs varied wildly. And, as we shall see, they still do.

Certification (1970–1987)

During the late sixties, the RID was faced with the urgent problem of quality control in the provision of interpreting services. It became obvious that not every sign student who joined the RID with the required two sponsoring members could in fact function effectively as an interpreter.

The RID began a pilot program of certification tests in 1970, which became official in 1972. Local teams composed of three certified hearing interpreters and two certified deaf relay interpreters were trained to evaluate new candidates on their skill in interpreting from video between English and either ASL or Signed English. Candidates received certificates for "interpreting" between ASL and English or for "transliterating" between English and Signed English. Evaluations for oral interpreters in lipreading and mouthing were also instituted but later dropped.

The term *transliterating* may be a little strange to our French colleagues who have no equivalent term, so it may be worth a rather lengthy digression to explain what we mean. The term is still used today to refer to fairly literal translations between English and Signed English. Some of our deaf clients, especially at the university level, have specifically requested transliterating, and the establishment of a transliterating certificate reflected this demand (it must be admitted that even some deaf people not comfortable with Signed English had to make do with transliterating because, as we have seen, the newer interpreters had never really been taught American Sign Language).

"Transliteration" even received some scientific justification based on the theory that Signed English was part of a continuum of signing alternatives that included "pure" ASL, on one end, and very "English-like" signing, on the other. According to the theory, any signing that was not on the "pure" ASL end was a pidgin combination of ASL and English, and, in fact, this so-called Pidgin Signed English was known for many years as PSE.

Further "legitimation" of the use of Signed English and transliteration came from the educational establishment. Not content with the natural mixing of ASL and English that had been in use among some deaf people for years, educators proliferated artificial sign systems designed specifically to teach English to deaf children visually. While this attempt proved in the end to be a dismal failure, it did add to the push for Signed English in the seventies and eighties.

There are still deaf people who regularly use an English-like variety of signing. There may be many reasons for this. It may be the result of decades of insistence by the hearing majority that ASL is inferior to English; it may be that some deaf people simply prefer Signed English in certain situations; or it may even be that some deaf people trust their own understanding of hearing culture more than they trust an interpreter's ability to interpret to deaf culture. Whatever the case, the question is moot for the interpreter on the job. Interpreters should respect the feelings of their clients and adapt their interpretation to accommodate them.

Rather than categorizing deaf people into "pure" language users and Signed English users according to the outdated pidgin theory, it might be more practical for the interpreter to think of ASL as a multifaceted language that has "borrowed" freely from the majority language that surrounds it. Personally, I do not believe in a "pure" ASL any more than I believe in a "pure" English.

Our French colleagues certainly have experience in the arguments on both sides of the "language purity" issue. French purists have long argued that the so-called *franglais* invasion of English words into French is contaminating the purity of French. And, since the seventeenth century, thanks to Cardinal Richelieu, there is a French Academy charged with monitoring the language. But the truth is, of course, that languages that are in contact will inevitably influence each other. And people who are bilingual in English and French will pepper their speech in one language with words from the other, and even jump from English to French from one sentence to the next. Bilinguals in ASL and English, or in LSF and French, of course, do the same thing, depending on how bilingual they and their interlocutors are. Most signers in the United States and in France, after all, are bilingual to some degree.

Maybe if we in the United States had avoided the arbitrary sign systems of the seventies and eighties, we could have avoided some of the divisiveness we now see in the deaf and hearing communities regarding the use of ASL versus Signed English. Artificial tampering with any language is bound to provoke an outcry. Language purists or "language police" serve a useful function in the public debate about language use (William Safire's weekly column on English usage in the *New York Times Magazine* is a case in point), but ASL purists in our interpreting community are just as important.

In any case, for better or worse, interpreters in the United States are still tested and certified in both interpreting and transliterating, even, as we shall see, under the revised certification system instituted in 1989.

The Struggle for a Professional Identity: The Role of the Interpreter

Our views of the precise role of a professional interpreter have been in constant evolution. By the 1970s, as our professional awareness grew, we began to distance ourselves from the old model of the interpreter "*for* the Deaf," as helper and even adviser with a "duty" to the deaf community. We began instead to demand professional independence and to insist that we police ourselves through the national professional association with a certification process for interpreters and a grievance process for consumers of our services.

We began to think of the professional interpreter in terms of what we now call the "machine model," sometimes called the "conduit" model: the interpreter simply transmits the message without adding or subtracting anything, *never* intervenes, and has no effect on the outcome of the meeting interpreted. In part, this conception of the interpreter originated with a widespread misinterpretation of the strict neutrality demanded by the code of ethics. Even those interpreters who were becoming fluent in ASL sometimes had problems interpreting the *sense* of a meeting for fear of adding to or subtracting from the message. In fact, the concept of the machine model "interpreter" only reinforced the trend toward sign-for-word transliterating using Signed English and even awkward word-for-sign English gloss transliterations rather than really interpreting between ASL and English.

The "machine model" couldn't adequately describe the interpreter's role. Interpreting is an incredibly complex process and, of course, involves more than merely translating signs into words or words into signs.

So, by the mid-1970s, we began to speak of ourselves as "communication facilitators." We certainly recognized that we needed to be sensitive to the needs of our consumers, both hearing and deaf, but we had a hard time defining exactly what linguistic "adjustments" needed to be made in the interpreting process for our consumers to really understand each other.

In the early 1980s the trend was toward a bilingual/bicultural (sometimes referred to as BiBi) model of interpreting. Our major goal in interpreting was and is the transmission of *meaning* and *intent* from one language to another. This goal may include not only linguistic but also cultural adjustments in our interpretations.

Even before an assignment, we need to prepare ourselves. We need to ask, What is the context of the meeting? How many people? Who are they? Have they worked with interpreters before or might we need to clarify our role beforehand? In what kind of room will the meeting take place? Might special lighting be needed? What will the content be? Might there be a particular jargon used or will they be talking about a subject we can get background information on? What variety of ASL or of English might the speakers use?

Then, of course, during the assignment, we must faithfully interpret the content: not only the speaker's words or signs, but the meaning and intent as well. In addition, we must render it in the language register that corresponds to the context and the setting, adapting our interpretation to accommodate the needs of the speakers.

Very recently, the idea of the interpreter as "ally" has found some support among interpreters who are politically active. An interpreter acting as ally will recognize that there is an imbalance of power between most hearing and deaf people who are communicating through an interpreter. The interpreter-as-ally will try to make up for this inequity by encouraging the empowerment of the deaf person involved.

Actually, these different "models" of interpreting may not be mutually exclusive. They determine behaviors that may all be useful in different situations with different clients who have different backgrounds and different expectations about the meeting in which the interpreter will be working. Again, the one constant in our role as interpreters is to accommodate the needs of the speakers in a given situation.

In addition, the interpreter's role as a professional vis-à-vis the deaf community has always been a delicate issue. On a daily basis we deal with members of a minority community who have suffered and still suffer from blatant discrimination and injustice. Some of our clients, both hearing and deaf, may even still expect us to help and advise deaf people. The discussions provoked by the "interpreter-as-ally" proponents are important, but it is a very delicate situation when we are interpreting and at the same time *advocating* for deaf people. I know that this is a big issue in France, where the rights of deaf people are routinely trampled on, even more so than in the United States. But we need to be very careful that all our clients see our behavior as fair and honest.

Our professional identity also involves the role of our professional association in representing our interests. For most of its first two decades, power in the RID was held mainly by the board of directors. In 1983 the association was restructured to require that decisions be made by the membership. We are just beginning to come to terms with the ramifications of that important change: in a voluntary professional association, members must take seriously their participation in voting and in committee work if the RID is to move forward. In a group as diverse as ours it may not be easy for every member to live with the decisions made by the entire membership. Recently, the issue of recertification under the new RID system, as we shall see, caused particularly heated debates.

The New Certification System (1989–Present)

In 1987, RID testing was discontinued for two years while new tests were developed. It had become obvious that the old system, though recognized by law in some states, had to be revised or replaced. Rising complaints from the deaf community, coupled with an increasing awareness that standardized tests had to be scientifically validated, prodded the RID to develop the new tests. The old evaluation, more or less a family affair, was probably the best we could do at a time when we had little experience training and evaluating interpreters. The new tests, developed at great cost and after two years of intensive preparation, involved written and video prototypes, field testing with interpreters from various backgrounds, statistical analysis to determine the validity and reliability of written test items, membership evaluation of prototype video materials (the members voted on the acceptable minimum skill level to pass the test), training of evaluators (whose interreliability is and will be constantly checked), and so forth. The new certificates became available starting in 1989. We think we now have a test that reliably measures skill in interpreting.

In 1991, the RID had 3,733 members, of whom 2,070 were certified at one level or another, under either the old system or the new. Of the certified interpreters, 123 were deaf people certified as relay interpreters.

As the old certificates expired, interpreters were to be tested under the new system in order to remain certified. In 1991, however, RID members voted to extend all the old certificates indefinitely. The result: for the rest of this generation, we will be explaining an alphabet soup of some twenty different levels and kinds of certification, most of which are not even being offered any more, to confused clients, employers, and legislators. Obviously, a majority of our certified members did not want to be retested. Some complained that the new test was too expensive; others that the RID had made promises to them that they would never have to be retested. This decision by the membership may affect our credibility as a self-policing professional association. But only time will tell.

Some members are suggesting that the RID should eventually hand over responsibility for all evaluation and testing to an independent testing service with experience and expertise in testing and licensing, and let the RID and NAD serve as consultants to the testing professionals. Hispanic, African-American and Asian-American interpreters, however, have reasons to be concerned about the bias against minorities in the records of many of those testing services.

Meanwhile, many members are concerned about the proliferation of other less formal interpreter evaluation and screening mechanisms. State agencies dealing with deafness, the NAD, and even local groups are developing competing evaluation systems. Because of the continuing shortage of interpreters, they frequently include levels of "passing" scores that have lower competence requirements than the RID test in order to encourage more new interpreters to enter the market.

Historically, the problem of certification has consumed much of RID's resources. Continuing problems result from the fact that some of us have not been clear about exactly what a certification system can and cannot do, what it is, and what it is not.

Certification is important, as a doctor's license or a driver's license is important, but it must be emphasized that certification denotes only a *minimum* competency to practice, not advanced standing in the field. If the RID standard is indeed considered a minimum competency by the majority of interpreters and deaf people, then the proliferation of screening tests with less stringent criteria should be a grave concern to both interpreters and deaf people.

By the same token, RID certification does not mean that the interpreter can function in every situation or in every setting. Our clients must learn to choose interpreters judiciously, and interpreters must learn to accept or reject assignments for work depending on their skills and on the setting and the content of the meeting. After all, not all doctors can do brain surgery, not all drivers can enter the Indianapolis 500, and not all interpreters can interpret at the United Nations.

As I interpret with increasing frequency at high-level international conferences, I am exposed to many models of spoken language interpreters who work in the booths interpreting between French, English, and Spanish. I used to think of those interpreters as almost faultless— they certainly have access to some extraordinary training programs and are highly paid. Surprisingly, though, the quality of their work is often sadly lacking. While conferees *do* sometimes complain, audiences usually understand the limits and inconveniences of working long hours with information filtered through interpreters, and they make certain concessions. Conscientious interpreters will continually strive to improve their interpreting, but no training system or certification process will ever ensure perfection.

Interpreter Training

There are probably about seventy-five different training programs in the United States, most of them evening classes or two-year programs. In 1979 interpreter trainers established the Conference of Interpreter Trainers (CIT) to provide a forum for exchanges and the development of curricula. The CIT, in conjunction with the RID, has just completed a project to establish standards for training programs in the United States. Eventually, such programs should be evaluated and accredited as professional training programs. Without standards and accreditation in both ASL programs and interpreter-training programs at the university level, our claims to professionalism rest on shaky ground.

Training of interpreters in ASL and English has suffered from the lack of truly bilingual applicants who enter training programs. In most of these programs, the students spend too much time simply gaining fluency in the languages, and not enough time learning and practicing the actual process of interpreting. We are not even close to the elaborate training programs offered to the spoken language interpreters who work international conferences, United Nations meetings, and regional meetings such as the European Parliament. New sign-language interpreters graduating from training programs in the United States are still woefully unprepared for the interpreting market.

Solving the Current Crisis

The biggest problem we face today in both France and the United States is a crisis in confidence. Both deaf and hearing people must have confidence in the quality of interpreting services. The issue of who "controls" interpreters and their certification has been often discussed in both countries. Because deaf people have traditionally been excluded from positions of power in society, they now rightfully claim decision-making power in matters that concern them. Talk is rife in both countries about deaf people "taking over" interpreting services, and interpreters themselves, who serve both hearing and deaf people, are caught in the middle.

Deaf people should certainly have the right to monitor and control the teaching of their own language and the dissemination of information about their culture. If deaf people in France and in the United States truly work to ensure that sign-language teaching and information about deafness is efficient and accurate, then learners of LSF and ASL can become truly fluent and culturally aware, and the new recruits for the interpreting profession will be truly ready for specific training in interpreting.

Interpreters and interpreter trainers, both hearing and deaf, will have to work to ensure that they never stop improving their skills. Only by working together can we collaboratively solve the current crisis.

We will all have an influence on the climate in which interpreting takes place—positively or negatively.

Consumers of interpreting services, both deaf and hearing, can have a negative influence by abusing interpreters: complaining about interpreters' "taking advantage" of deaf people by getting paid, refusing to acknowledge the interpreter's need for adequate preparation time before an assignment, and ignoring interpreters' demands for proper working conditions (breaks are necessary for the muscles as well as the mind, and interpreters working in twos and threes for long meetings is no longer a luxury). Of course, deaf people can exert a positive influence also: by constantly improving the teaching of sign language, campaigning for public information on deafness, educating consumers about how to use interpreters effectively, and lobbying for their legal right to interpreting services.

As interpreters we can have a negative impact by not working constantly to improve our skills, by discriminating against deaf people, even unconsciously (an eye gaze turned away even for an instant can discourage a deaf participant from taking his turn speaking in a meeting), by not acting in a strictly ethical manner on every job, and so forth. Or we can have a positive impact by constantly striving to be better and more articulate interpreters, by being clear about our role, by advocating for better working conditions so that we *can* work at our full potential, and, of course, by respecting the capabilities, the values, and the opinions of our clients, both hearing and deaf.

The United States is no paradise for either deaf people or for interpreters, but we have made great strides in the past twenty-five years: Deaf people enjoy more access to higher education and a greater variety of intellectual and cultural events than ever before. Interpreting is a delicate and difficult business. If we want to attract bright young people to interpreting as a career, we must overcome our current difficulties and establish ourselves as respected professionals.

The National Association for Interpretation in Sign Language

RACHID MIMOUN

The National Association for Interpretation in Sign Language (ANPILS) has been an important activist organization by and for the deaf since the birth of deaf action movements during the early 1980s. During the past twelve years, as concepts of interpretation have changed in France, so has the association, which has altered both its nature and its name several times.

Hearing persons speaking on behalf of the deaf were the first to begin to define the interpreting profession. They set up the French National Association of Interpreters for the Hearing-Impaired (ANFIDA). They started from scratch in creating this pioneering organization. The use of the term "hearing impaired" demonstrates that they aimed at the entire population of people with hearing deficits. The interpreters tried to become qualified in all the many communications media used by the highly diverse population of hearing-impaired people, including signed French, French Sign Language (LSF), mouthed French, note-taking displayed by overhead projectors, cued speech, and so on. These methods were so varied and contradictory that it proved impossible to establish training courses enabling one person to master them all. Instead, training focused on a knowledge of the hearing impaired and their "psychology," to the exclusion of training in communication methods. Moreover, the pre-

Rachid Mimoun is president of the National Association for Interpretation in Sign Language (Association Nationale pour l'Interprétation en Langue des Signes).

dominant attitude of many early interpreters was that they were there to "help" the deaf.

The Two Languages for One Education association (2 LPE) brought about a major change when it organized training courses in sign language. The regular participation of professional conference interpreters and the emphasis placed on quality helped recast the definition of interpretation, which now came to mean the transformation from one language to another and from one culture to another. It then became necessary to divide the needs of the deaf population into two categories: aides to communication in French (mouthing, cued speech, note-taking) and interpretation between LSF and French. Since each category had different requirements, a clear distinction had to be drawn between their functions and training.

When ANFIDA decided to specialize in interpretation between the two languages, it changed its name to ANILS, the National Association of Sign Language Interpreters. This body consisted mostly of hearing persons, largely interpreters or trainee interpreters, and an active minority of deaf persons. The association promoted a code, defining the ethical and moral rules of the profession, including neutrality, confidentiality, and faithful transmission of the message, which became an integral part of the bylaws. The association helped foster the recognition of interpretation through lectures, courses, meetings with officials, and advice on the setting up of interpretation services.

At that juncture, an organization called SERAC (Sourds Entendants Recherche Action Communication/Deaf Hearing Research Action Communication) was set up that had as one aim the creation of fifteen-month interpreter-training courses. The two associations had strained relations that engendered mistrust by many members of the deaf community, who wondered why a new organization was created when the trend had been to combine existing ones. Some time was needed to find a workable cooperative arrangement, and meanwhile a shortage of funds and uncertainty about the future of the two organizations helped reduce the level of militancy.

Perhaps even more significant, ANILS members began to sense a growing gap between knowledge of interpretation by the hearing and by the deaf. The deaf, as a community, found themselves unable to select interpreters from their own members to communicate with the world. To create a balance and to establish complete trust between interpreters and deaf users of interpretation it was essential that the deaf have their say in the future of the profession.

On the basis of a membership referendum, the bylaws were amended to require that deaf persons would constitute a majority of the board of directors. This led to the creation of ANPILS. Interpreters remained important in the association as a source of information based on their personal experiences. The association, which now has approximately a hundred members, is less a group of interpreters than a group of people concerned with interpretation. Their main task is to gain recognition for the profession.

A deaf person chairs the board as guarantor to the deaf community that decisions regarding the profession are well founded. The interpreter members act as advisers and participate in all decisions that affect their profession.

ANPILS managed the interpretation services at the International Symposium on Sign Language held in Poitiers in July 1990. This was tantamount to a vote of confidence in the organization by the deaf community. The goals were high-quality services managed entirely by a deaf person and providing the first French deaf interpreters responsible for interpretation between French Sign Language and Signed Language. (Signed Language, known in English as International Sign, is common at international conferences.)

A series of roundtable discussions on various subjects have provided valuable exchanges of information among translators. One session addressed the training of translators; another dealt with professional issues. A "Roundtable on the Future" led ANPILS to formulate the organizing principles for its activities. In general, the organization regards itself as the interface between the deaf community and interpretation projects. It will assist in the training of interpreters and services at the *département* level. It will manage interpretation services for symposia and conferences, in keeping with the principles used for the symposium at Poitiers, and it will join in developing an experimental training program and in assessing students trained at SERAC. The association will cooperate with the Postgraduate School of Interpreters and Translators (ESIT) in Paris to establish a training course. The association believes that France should have four or five interpretation training centers working in cooperation under the auspices of universities.

This program will become effective only when national law recognizes sign language. The profession cannot develop until the deaf are recognized as having their own culture and their own language.

Interpreting in Criminal Cases in France

CHRISTIANE FOURNIER

The importance of interpreting for the deaf is largely unrecognized, not only by the general public but also by judges and by many of our hearing colleagues who practice translation or interpreting of foreign languages. This lack of knowledge can generate highly varied reactions toward both interpretation and the interpeter. I would like to lift the veil of ignorance by showing that our interpreting work rests on the same underlying principle as any other form of interpretation, which is "to understand in order to enable others to understand." In the courts, our role is the same as that of other interpreters, regardless of the languages employed. The linguistic obstacles we encounter arise from differences in social and cultural backgrounds between the speaker and the receiver. These are problems everyone has to deal with, but they are our daily lot and have an amplifying effect on the problems of interpretation in criminal cases.

Background

What does "interpretation" mean to the public at large? Probably most people regard it as the ability to juggle with words, in going from one language to another; it is some sort of gift shared by conference interpreters, court interpreters, liaison interpreters, and museum interpreter-guides. Some kinds of interpretation carry more visibility

---

Christiane Fournier is a sign-language interpreter, professor, and expert court translator.

or prestige than others, some carry less. The interpreter who serves the great personages of the time acquires more renown than the interpreter who works for the state prisons.

In fact, no form of interpretation is more "noble" than another, whatever the circumstances. There is good and bad interpretation, just as there are good and bad interpreters. Quality interpretation implies a level of professional skill available only through high-level training. Users of interpretation are entitled to expect this level of skill.

Interpretation is a form of communication practiced by a person acting as a mediator between two speakers who do not share a common language. A message consists of linguistic signs. Speech expresses an intention whose meaning cannot be reduced to the sum of the linguistic meanings that the language attributes to the words used. The meaning derives from a synthesis of linguistic meanings and of contextual knowledge accumulated since the beginning of the speech.

Let me quote the following sentence, taken out of context. In the judge's chambers, a young woman said to me: "This lady took my baby." The sentence is easily translated linguistically but can be properly reexpressed only at a semantic level. "Took" could mean "kidnapped," "seized," "took away," "placed with a foster mother." What was the actual context? Was it dramatic? Was it an everyday event? All this information is vital to the interpreter's attempt to follow the thread of the speech.

Through a process of appropriation, the interpreter uses not only linguistic knowledge but extralinguistic knowledge: place, circumstances, personality of the speaker. The interpreter goes beyond the words heard in order to apprehend the intentions of the speaker, and deverbalizes the speech to feel free to choose the most appropriate equivalent expressions in the target language. The processed message should produce the same effects on the addressee as the original message.

Interpretation is not a form of transcoding but an intelligible, faithful reformulation of the original discourse. Should we distinguish between conference interpreting and criminal interpreting, inasmuch as interpretation remains interpretation and the skills needed for quality work are identical in each case? While skills should be the same in the two fields of interpretation, the role of the interpreter, the working conditions, the linguistic obstacles, and the frequently delicate and upsetting human situations all require special abilities and call for strategies adapted to the circumstances.

Criminal Court Interpretation

On entering the courtroom, accused persons often feel anguish and concern about the outcome of the case or are embarrassed at the idea of having private matters laid open in public. The accused who do not speak French share these feelings in addition to the fear of not understanding what is being said and of not being understood. The deaf accused have even greater anxiety. The fact that they are of French nationality tends to obscure the need for an interpreter: the uninitiated do not always realize the need. Hence the agony of the deaf accused if they see that no interpreter has been summoned. How will they know when their names are called? They can't hear the words, whereas hearing foreigners could at least hear their names. The eyes of the deaf accused will be riveted on the usher's face to lip-read their names when they are spoken. If location in the courtroom makes this impossible, they will seek other indications.

My role as interpreter begins as soon as I have handed my summons to the usher. My first task is to contact the accused in an absolutely objective spirit, harboring no feelings of pity or anything else. The accused is relieved to see me, as I can tell from facial expressions. This initial contact, established ideally before the court proceedings begin, contributes to improving communication and offers an opportunity to learn about the mode of communication used by the deaf person. These preliminaries are part of the interpreter's preparatory work.

When the case is called, and before any examinations begin, the interpreter must find the courtroom location that ensures that the message will be well heard and clearly seen. The interpreter must be almost facing the accused—and not side by side as the spoken-language interpreter is normally placed—and must at all costs avoid turning his or her back to the light. If the interpreter has not previously met with the accused, it is necessary to determine the accused's mode of communication. Various modes may be used, depending on the degree of deafness and the educational background. The court always allows this short preliminary exchange in the interest of good interpretation. The interpreter needs to ascertain whether he or she can provide communication between the accused and the court. Should this be impossible, the interpreter must inform the court, which will make a decision about what to do.

The modes of speech used depend on the context and the personality of the accused. The presiding judge may ask the accused to address the court directly; the interpreter must inform the accused of this request. At different stages of the hearing, speakers may change. A hearing person can hear the speaker's voice and turn in the proper direction. Even if the words are not understood, the accused can associate the words with the right speaker. The deaf person cannot do this, and so the interpreter must always explain who is speaking by indicating the speaker before beginning to interpret the message.

To understand a message, the interpreter requires both linguistic and extralinguistic (legal and contextual) knowledge. The interpreter must have relevant information about the case. However, these facts are seldom communicated even when the interpreter so requests. Is this owing to fear of partiality during the interpretation or to the fact that the request is simply considered pointless? I don't know. I've been told, "You won't have any special problem, you just have to translate." Why then is it so necessary to have a minimum amount of information? The judges know the facts of the case, and the accused is very much concerned with them. Their shared knowledge can permit communication based on certain implicit terms. But an interpreter who lacks the shared knowledge may have to grope for the underlying sense of the message, particularly at the outset, and may therefore not transmit a sufficiently intelligible message. Ideally, the interpreter has already been involved in written interrogations for the case and thus has some basic information about it. In reality that is often not the ease.

Once, in a case where a deaf person was accused of assault and battery, I had some of these very difficulties. After establishing the identity of the accused, which raised no problem, the court asked the accused to give his version of the facts. He said, in literal translation, "It isn't my fault, my boss fault, him do nothing, I don't like mock, me-deaf." Lacking contextual data, I could do no more than formulate hypotheses about the meaning. Who was this "boss"? His employer? The owner of a private establishment or a public one? Was the boss doing the mocking? I decided to ask a question—a method I will explain below when discussing strategies—in order to get the basic facts.

The content of a message is not restricted to the notional aspect. Apart from some purely informational technical discourse, where emotion would be out of place, the emotional aspect is an integral part of the message. Particularly in the courtroom, every statement is overlaid with the speaker's feelings: intonation for the hearing, facial expression for the deaf. Facial expression is to sign language what prosody is to spoken languages. The voice betrays fear, shame, anger, affection, irony.

Given the interpreter's officially neutral position in the proceedings, what kind of voice should be employed? I feel that using a neutral voice is tantamount to taking a stand, and that by doing so one may give the impression that the accused is indifferent to the case or situation. Using a neutral tone betrays the intended discourse of the accused because the reformulation will not have the same impact on the hearer as the original message would have. Speaking the same words with a different intonation does not communicate the same intended message.

The speaker is responsible for his or her statements, including not only the words chosen but also the intonation. A failure to reproduce intonation is a failure to objectively convey the meaning of the message. I am not saying that the translator should exaggerate the phrasing and rhythm of the original in an attempt to recreate the mental reservations or hidden motives of the speaker. An interpreter who did so would exceed the proper role. The interpreter must stick to the message, the whole message, and nothing but the message.

Rhythm can also provide information. A person accused of public indecency relates the facts at an accelerated pace and without the slightest pause, perhaps out of shame or embarrassment or from fear that an acquaintance or relative may understand what is being communicated. I, as the interpreter, search for explanations as a matter of exegesis and am not personally involved in my interpretation. I am, however, obliged to adopt the same pace of speaking, since the rhythm will produce the same effect as the original on the court. In simultaneous translation, I have sometimes tried to follow the same flow as the original "speech." If my words sound rushed, my rate of speech emulates the rapid pace of the signs and gestures.

Interpretation Techniques

The choice of interpretation mode varies with the different phases of the hearing: examination, statement of facts, indictment, and pleading. The questions asked to establish the accused's identity are very specific and need only brief answers. Since questions and answers are brief, the preferred mode of communication would be consecutive translations. Once the judge requests the accused to relate the facts, the replies will require some development and the consecutive mode will no longer suffice. Watching a speaker without understanding him or her may irritate the court. Gaps in the relaying of the message may create a feeling of unease and lengthen the proceedings. Sentence-by-sentence consecutive translation is also to be discouraged, since it interferes with the speech rhythms and may prevent the accused from following the thread of meaning.

I prefer simultaneous interpretation at this stage. Use of simultaneous translation eliminates the lag between original discourse and interpretation and permits the accused to communicate through signs (in the linguistic sense of the term), to which are added facial expressions, the amplitude of gestures, a certain style of behavior—all of which are important linguistic and psychological contributions. The court perceives the entire statement, including all these aspects, through the interpreter. Compared to our colleagues who practice spoken languages, we interpreters of the deaf do not have to superimpose our voice on the original, which greatly facilitates the use of simultaneous interpretation in the courtroom.

Occasionally the interpreter must listen to the first one or two sentences before beginning to relay the message, a method known as "semiconsecutive." The interpreter must gauge the right moment to reformulate statements while the accused continues uninterrupted. The court sometimes asks for a sight translation of a document, such as police report, a medical analysis, or the like. Depending on the type of text and its length, the translator's lack of prior knowledge about the material may hinder a valid interpretation. The court may ask for a summary of the text without realizing that such a request may not necessarily be fair to the accused.

The indictment and the pleading are interpreted simultaneously. Audible to everyone in the courtroom, these presentations by the prosecuting and defense attorneys are intended for judges and are not always fully understood by the public. The presentations contain two linguistic registers. The first, part of the legal "technolect," or jargon, refers to the criminal code and legal precedents; the second, which is part of the "sociolect," is a language of the same sociocultural category used to discuss a particular version of the facts. The sociolect and technolect each oblige the interpreter to adopt specific strategies. In the first case, the interpreter will adapt the register of the attorneys to the language level or register used by the defendant, in order to convey the basic message. In the second case, since sign languages have a lexical void in the area of legal terminology, the interpreter must adopt an extremely didactic approach.

Deafness-linked Problems

A few comments about deafness will clarify the various interpretation strategies. A certain amount of confusion arises from the variety of terms used to designate the deaf: deaf and dumb, deaf, hearing impaired. We are not always consistent in applying these terms, using them sometimes to distinguish among medical characteristics and sometimes as synonyms. "Deaf and dumb," ancient and archaic, has a highly negative connotation that conveys the image of a person with a handicap and with low intellectual ability. In strictly medical terms, deaf mutes do exist, but they represent only a few isolated cases. It is easy to picture the surprise—sometimes the stupefaction—of the court when a defendant presented as a deaf mute speaks intelligibly and with a fair mastery of French.

"Deaf" covers a greater range and is used for the severely deaf, whether born deaf or deafened in early childhood. "Hearing impaired" applies to people of average deafness and, more especially, to those who became deaf as adults and who refuse to be called deaf. They are entirely different from "the deaf" and rarely benefit from our assistance as interpreters.

The varying degrees of deafness, the varying levels of education, and the differing sociocultural environments require the interpreter to choose from among modes of communication ranging from sign language (a clearly codified language) to more or less sophisticated pidgin languages, right down to the most rudimentary forms of miming. Some deaf persons combine signed communication with lipreading, while others use lipreading alone. The interpreter must have a variety of skills and be able to adapt to different situations. The most difficult case, for the interpreter, is that of the deaf defendant who communicates in a foreign language or who is alingual, that is, has no mother tongue, no sign language. In such cases we must mime. Any person of normal intelligence tries to communicate with other human beings, but the absence of a shared linguistic code is a major hindrance to conceptualization and abstract thought.

When the defendant is capable only of mimic language and the case relates to public indecency, rape, incest, or some similar offense, the translator and the court confront an especially delicate situation. Languages have sufficiently explicit vocabularies to describe the facts. The more reprehensible the facts, however, the further the terms used are removed from everyday speech, thus throwing a veil of modesty over what is being described. In the absence of a linguistic code, the presiding judge's questions can be interpreted to the defendant only through mime, which can cause extreme embarrassment to inexperienced interpreters, especially when they sense all eyes in the courtroom are fastened on them. Special arrangements need to be made in such cases.

When the defendant lacks a means of communication apart from mime or mimic language—as with the case of foreign alingual deaf persons—the interpreter has a very hard time indeed. We may try various strategies to assist comprehension, such as employing analogies or descriptions, but we remain in a very concrete field or within the domain of the defendant's experience. As a last resort, the court may ask a family member to communicate with the accused. That kind of interpretation lacks impartiality and is therefore not valid according to professional standards.

Specific Aspects

The interpreter functions as a mediator, a communicator who must place a foreigner or a deaf person on the same level of communication as a native speaker or a hearing person. The obligations and the limits of the function define the translator's role. The interpreter must faithfully and impartially transmit the entire message. I could dwell at length on the meaning of "faithfully." Faithful to whom? To what? Faithful to the words in the original message? (Only a nonprofessional could believe that!) The interpreter must be faithful to the message, to the words the speaker intended to say and faithful to the impression the speaker wished to convey. The interpreter must show neutrality toward the defendant, the court, and the case, expressing no personal opinion and neither approving nor disapproving of what is said. Any emotions in the interpreter's voice are merely reproducing the emotions of the speaker.

The interpreter must not slip into the role of teacher, moralizer, or advocate. It is all too easy to cross the line, the best proof of this found in the fact that some defendants will judge the interpreter's skill according to whether the verdict is favorable or not.

From the outset of the hearing, the interpreter should introduce each of the judges of the court and state clearly that he or she is merely the interpreter and is obliged to transmit everything that the defendant says. The interpreter thus avoids being placed in an awkward position if the defendant should choose to slip in a few insults on the assumption that the interpreter will not translate them.

The interpreter should always speak in the first person on behalf of the speaker. This means constantly changing roles between defendant and judge, and makes for a true dialogue, while the use of the third person would create a filter in the communication process. The interpreter uses the third person only to indicate that he has something to say on his own behalf: "The interpreter would wish to inform you that . . ."

At a conference, the speaker and the audience share the same background knowledge, and the speaker will use the appropriate linguistic register. The conference interpreter transmits the message—or the image, I prefer to say—on the same wavelength. In the courts, linguistic obstacles make the interpreter a tightrope walker, who must use two different levels as support while being obliged to transmit the message. In each case, the interpreting process is the same—"Understand in order to enable others to understand"—but linguistic obstacles force the interpreter to employ certain strategies that place the speaker and listener on the same wavelength. The defendants are far from having as much knowledge as the judges, and I am not referring solely to legal matters.

The differences in cultural levels can have serious implications. "Nobody is supposed to be unaware of the law," but concepts of good and evil underlie our laws, our moral values, our education. Language is the vector enabling us to acquire these concepts. Failure to master spoken and written French owing to educational shortcomings leads to divergent sets of values. Some defendants are unable to understand the criminal nature of receiving stolen goods, particularly if it has been done in the name of friendship, nor can they comprehend that the police are legally entitled to search their home if they have a warrant.

Linguistic obstacles go hand-in-hand with differences in cultural level. Some defendants have a limited stock of words. This requires the interpreter to guess at the meaning of the words and the message. For example, the sign corresponding to "woman" can also refer to a wife, mother, daughter, or sister. Only context can clarify the meaning, but often it does not.

The interpreter must formulate hypotheses about the meaning, particularly if he or she has no knowledge of the facts of the case. However, the interpreter cannot remain in a hypothetical flux but must advise the court of the communication difficulty and get additional information from the presiding judge. To return to the sentence I quoted at the beginning, "This is the lady who took my baby," when I heard it I formulated two hypotheses. The lady in question, probably a social worker, either obtained an abortion for the young woman or placed the infant with a foster family. A short question-and-answer session enabled me to understand that the infant had been placed in an institution. The experience had been very painful for the mother, which explains her use of the verb "to take or remove."

The second statement I quoted earlier is a series of non sequiturs: "It isn't my fault, my boss fault, him do nothing, I don't like mock, me-deaf." I could not transform this jumble into an intelligible message. Once again, through a series of questions, this time asked by the presiding judge, it was possible to create a coherent statement that represented what the defendant was trying to convey. By asking what had happened, who were the protagonists, and when it had happened, the judge and interpreter were able to arrive at a logical statement that contained no problems of understanding.

If the interpreter is not faithful to the words, that is, does not interpret word for word, he or she must remain faithful to the linguistic register of the speaker, which reflects the personality of the speaker. Sometimes, however, it is necessary to adapt the message. Often the linguistic register is colloquial and may contain slang. Occasionally vulgar expressions are used, which is not to the defendant's advantage. The interpreter must decide whether the vulgarity is deliberate or comes from a lack of language skill or a difference in register. Consider this example.

Presiding judge to defendant: "What is going to happen to your wife?"
Defendant to judge: "I couldn't give a f——."

The defendant had no intention of provoking the court. Why then should the interpreter draw the ire of the court, since the effect would exceed the intent of the message? However, the interpreter should not go too far in the other direction and use elevated language like "I don't feel concerned." I translated it, "Makes no difference to me," a colloquial enough expression showing indifference, rather than "I couldn't care less," which is ironic.

The interpreter plays an informative role for the court and must take the initiative in providing information to the judges when that seems necessary. Imagine that the judge says to the defendant, "Calm down, you're very agitated." A hearing person, the judge, perceives the defendant's facial agitation as a nervous state, whereas it is in fact connected to an issue of linguistic skill. The less skilled a deaf person is in sign language, the more he or she will compensate through increasingly ample or excited gestures. The interpreter who provides this insight to the court helps the defendant's behavior be judged more fairly.

Conclusion

Article 345 of the Code of Criminal Procedure states that if the accused is "a deaf mute" and unable to write, the judge should appoint as an interpreter "the person most accustomed to conversing with him. The same shall apply to a deaf mute witness." If the deaf person "is able to read and write," the court clerk should write the questions or comments and given them to the accused or the witness, who must then write his answers or statements.

I am aware of the problems that judges have in recruiting qualified interpreters, but a great deal of caution should be exercised regarding this law. "Accustomed to conversing with" is not synonymous with the ability to interpret. "Able to read and write" frequently means able to decipher a text and copy it. In either case, the meaning of the message will be unclear. If the court follows this law strictly, it could encounter big problems.

I would therefore like to suggest that in order to treat the accused fairly and to give full respect to the principles of justice, the law be amended to state that the interpreters must be qualified for court-room work.

Education for Deaf Children

The Language and Culture of the Deaf Community

PATRICK BELISSEN

The deaf community has almost no policymaking role in our system of education, and, conversely, the system of education does not take into consideration the essence of the deaf community: its language and culture. That is to say, the educational system was developed without the participation of deaf people and without any understanding of how deaf people live in their day-to-day lives. The medical profession has an all-powerful role in determining how the educational system works for the deaf. The lives of deaf people depend on physicians' skills, science, and expertise. Deaf people belong to them: the disease of hearing impairment must be treated, no matter what the cost. The medical profession also holds an omnipotent place in French social mores. At the slightest ache or pain, we run to the physician, and those who take full charge of their bodies and realize their full potential are rare indeed.

Where do the language and culture of deaf people fit into all that? In practice, they have no place in the training of physicians, no place even in the training of teachers, including those trained in special education. During the past few years, of course, the situation has improved somewhat: here and there people talk about French Sign Language (LSF). They mention deaf culture—but certainly not in medical schools, or at least not to my knowledge. And yet, society is beginning to recognize the importance of the body, which is no longer

---

Patrick Belissen is director of the training division of the French National Federation of the Deaf (Fédération Nationale des Sourds de France).

95

taboo. One has only to note the increase in the different methods of getting in touch with the body, some of which are only fads while others are becoming entrenched: aerobics, stretching, yoga, California massage, tai chi, martial arts, biofeedback, primal scream, and biodynamic psychology.

Sign language will certainly benefit from this changing relationship to the body. We are beginning to understand that to suppress the body's natural means of expression is detrimental, can have profound effects, and can stunt one's growth. It is becoming ever more obvious that to tie the hands of deaf people is to kill them, to prevent them from realizing their potential.

But—and there is always a "but"—there is oralism. Yes, it is fine for deaf people to speak with their hands, as long as their auditory deficiency is treated first and foremost and as long as they learn to speak. Why? The response is as irrefutable and obvious as the question is absurd and aberrant: to live, one must speak! Hearing people firmly believe that speaking is the sine qua non of social and economic integration. Without speech there is no salvation. This belief legitimizes the current institutional practices based on the primacy of oralism for the deaf. As a consequence, deaf people's language and culture are doomed to take second place in the priorities of the educational system. The reign of obscurantism, the mental block vis-à-vis the language and culture of the deaf by institutions charged with serving them, has caused untold misery in the collective consciousness of the deaf community.

What do deaf people think of all this? How many hearing professionals in the field take the trouble to ask them what they think of their education? Very few. Of course, deaf people do think for themselves, but the hearing person takes as the absolute reference point the ontogeny and phylogeny of *Homo hearing-sapiens,* which automatically makes hearing impairment a handicap affecting deaf people's thinking mechanisms. One needs to think for them, because hearing thinking is assumed to be superior to deaf thinking.

In other words, the educational system does not account for the intrinsic values of the deaf community, its language and its culture. I am not going to try to explain the language and culture of deaf people; I don't claim to be able to. And if I ask you to explain the language and culture of hearing people, you would be in as much of a bind as I am. In fact, I do not want to put deaf people on a dissection table. Their physical environment, and their system of perception, their way of integrating into the social environment, their language are all so complex that to reduce them to terms like "visual perception" or "gestural expression" shows an obvious ignorance of the realities of deafness. You cannot understand the difference between hearing and deaf with the intellect alone. To begin to understand the language and culture of deaf people, you must be open to this alternative perception of life, a life in which deaf people are emancipated from the omnipotence of the hearing.

Language and Culture in the Struggle for Empowerment

LAWRENCE R. FLEISCHER

In many ways, politics has helped shape the deaf community in today's world. One has to wonder to what extent, if any, have deaf people been aware of events affecting their lives. Considering the destructive cycle of nonachievement perpetuated in schools for the deaf, it is easy to answer "Not at all" to the question. It is my general observation that schools for the deaf have been slow in becoming sensitive to the special needs of deaf learners. Consequently these learners find their quest for knowledge stalemated, and instead of receiving the attention they need, they are labeled as disabled individuals in the world of learning, as passive recipients of knowledge. Clearly, such educational practices foster little opportunity for critical thinking.

While I trust my own instincts, I am fully cognizant that I should not accept everything that has been taught me as *true*. In addition, I shouldn't assume that the ideas of others are unbiased. Whether the idea is clear or vague, we always need to integrate it intelligently into the lives of deaf Americans.

More and more people have come to accept that American Sign Language (ASL) and other sign languages are, indeed, human languages. Acceptance of that fact has forced the deaf world, which has been deeply rooted in the pathological view of deafness, to face many new policies that concern them and need to be addressed. A clash between interest groups, including but not limited to deaf and non-

Lawrence R. Fleischer is professor of special education, School of Education, California State University at Northridge.

deaf communities, is inevitable—after all, the essence of politics lies in conflict. The resolution comes through coercion and manipulation or through bargaining and persuasion.

American Sign Language can be associated with significant political changes in the deaf community, including the push for deaf administrators in schools for the deaf and the incorporation of ASL in the classroom. In my paper I will illustrate a few grassroots actions directed at changing national policies for deaf people.

Much interest has arisen over the idea that Deaf (big "d") people represent membership in a community that is enriched by a heritage passed down from generation to generation. A distinction must be made between this group and deaf (small "d") people who do not have the same access to the deaf heritage. For example, some deaf people refuse to identify themselves as deaf people and shun deaf-community activities. Some are simply isolated and don't realize that there are other deaf people around. The means by which the deaf experience is internalized varies, and it can either be credited for one's fulfilling one's upbringing or blamed for one's unfair position in life. For both Deaf and deaf people, however, the underlying similarity is that access (or its denial) to the heritage determines one's entire existence.

Despite opposition by deaf people, diverse views such as oralism, cued speech, signed systems, and the like have been put forward as ideals that should shape the lives of deaf individuals. The result is a communications barrier, which has helped cheat deaf Americans out of many opportunities to experience life fully.

Examples that illustrate the general picture of the deaf movement in the domain of language and culture are limitless. Here are three brief instances.

Mixed Definition of ASL

In the good old days, before the turn of the century, deaf people across the country signed the same way—with dialectical variations, of course. Graduates of Gallaudet University, who entered various professions across the nation, assisted in standardizing language use.

By the early 1900s, misconceptions about the value of a signed language caused sign language to be devalued. Early linguists categorized signed language as "nonverbal communication"—which helped spread the belief that it wasn't a language at all!

Recently, some deaf faculty members at Gallaudet University, concerned about this definition of a signed language as proposed through ASL research, expressed disagreement with the ASL linguists. Their statement resulted in further confusion, which they adapted into a new definition of a signed language: it does include a "voice." The Gallaudet in-house definition of ASL is now vastly different from the current "scientific" worldview of signed language.

The Newest Revolution: "Unlocking the Curriculum"

The report "Unlocking the Curriculum: Principles for Achieving Access in Deaf Education," written in 1989 by three hearing authors (Robert Johnson, Scott Liddell, and Carol Erting), perceptively examines the poor achievement of deaf learners, the low expectations of deaf children, and the lack of equal access in deaf educational settings. Not only has it identified the reasons for academic failure by deaf children, but it has also offered a model program for their education that includes strategies for the acquisition of natural sign language.

The report differs with the conventional view that current teaching practices are adequate. Many professionals accuse the authors of having a political ideology. Nevertheless, in harmony with the concerns of the authors, alternative plans for bicultural/bilingual schools are now proliferating. Now that the forces of ASL have gained strength, a domino effect is influencing professional organizations, such as the Association of College Educators in Hearing Impairment and the Council on Education of the Deaf, to mention only two, and moving them to address the issues of poor academic achievement, low expectations, and lack of equal educational access.

Clearly, the level of consciousness had been raised as part of the political revolution. At this stage, a more appropriate slogan for the revolution would be "ASL for Deaf Education!"

Deaf Empowerment, Now and Later

The "Deaf President Now" movement that arose at Gallaudet University in 1988, when a new president had to be chosen, has had an enormous impact on deaf people all over the world. To make deaf people more aware of their common interests and to promote further changes, deaf leaders are encouraging greater involvement in professional organizations and activities that can have a direct impact on the lives of deaf people.

A situation that should concern all deaf people arose at my alma mater, the New York School for the Deaf. The controversy started when the school prevented a deaf teacher from teaching a preschool class because she could not speak intelligibly. The concern over the teacher's speaking ability by the school personnel tended to be reinforced by the parents of the children. But many deaf people question the value of such an emphasis on spoken language. For the sake of the deaf learners at the school, shouldn't the primary concern be the teacher's ability to interact and communicate with the students in their native language, ASL? How appropriate would it be, instead, to have a hearing teacher with limited ASL fluency?

Fortunately, an increasing number of deaf individuals are being exposed to empowerment and are taking on the responsibility of influencing society to change ridiculous situations like this one. But if they should fail to assume responsibility, they will only help perpetuate a status quo that puts deaf people in an unfavorable, unfair, and unequal position.

Conclusion

A political perspective definitely plays an important role in the language and culture of the deaf community, not only in the United States but all over the world. In order to cultivate awareness and inspire a greater commitment to the concerns of deaf people, we must have a greater sensitivity to political aspects of behavior.

As I write, events are creating obstacles to a true understanding of deaf people. The language policy now enforced to educate deaf children is heavily controlled by hearing and deaf (small "d") professionals, who resist the incorporation of ASL into the classroom because they think it will disrupt the acquisition of English. The professionals' own lack of ASL competence not only perpetuates this belief but denies deaf learners an appropriate role model.

Deaf people must constantly challenge the beliefs and acts aimed at taking political control over their language and education, until deaf people are satisfied with the results. At that point, a greater appreciation of deaf people will be realized.

Equality in Education

GERTRUDE S. GALLOWAY

The past decade has seen a considerable change in the way teachers in both regular and special education educate all children. Prior to 1975, most deaf children were placed and educated in state-owned or operated residential and special schools. Then came the enactment of two encompassing pieces of federal legislation governing the rights of the handicapped. Public Law 93-112, the Rehabilitation Act of 1973, includes a section (504) implying that no qualified handicapped person can be denied the benefits of any federally funded activity or program. Public Law 94-142, the Individuals with Disabilities Education Act (IDEA), states that a handicapped child is entitled to a free and appropriate public education. Handicapped children are now being identified in greater numbers. They receive more specialized attention and, in many cases, attend the same classes as nonhandicapped children, in public schools close to home.

The federal Education of the Deaf Act of 1986 (Title III of Public Law 99-371) established the Commission on Education for the Deaf. To fulfill its charge of studying "the quality of infant and early childhood education programs and of elementary, secondary, post-secondary, adult, and continuing education furnished to deaf individuals," the commission examined testimony and letters from children, parents, and educators. Commission members concluded that many deaf children were receiving inappropriate education or no education at all, the very same problem that prompted passage of the Education for All Handicapped Children Act (PL 94-142) in 1975.

Gertrude S. Galloway is superintendent of the Marie H. Katzenbach School for the Deaf in West Trenton, New Jersey.

Perhaps one reason for the disappointing level of education is the failure of "mainstreaming" to meet the expectations of those who have seen it as a way of serving many deaf children. As I understand the term, mainstreaming means the complete immersion of the student in a regular educational program with support services such as an interpreter or note-taker. In less than a decade, mainstreaming has become a common practice in public schools, and the percentage of deaf students in local public schools has increased greatly. Nevertheless, it is wrong to assume that these students are fully integrated into classes with hearing students and receive all the benefits of the regular classroom. Studies have indicated that many day students attend only physical education and art classes with hearing peers, yet the local school administration may describe them as mainstreamed. Furthermore, the classroom may be isolated at one end of the school building.

Aside from these deficiencies, it is not clear that mainstreaming is necessarily the best educational approach. I object to the implication that a deaf child is not normal unless mainstreamed with nonhandicapped children. My own view is that normalization, the principle underlying the mainstreaming concept, is often not the answer. For some deaf children, normalization may mean denial of the right to be different. "It is okay to be deaf" is the message we should be sending to all deaf children.

Reports about emotional and social difficulties raise other concerns. Deaf children learn best when they feel good about themselves, but reports from teachers at Gallaudet University suggest that students from mainstreamed settings tend to have trouble socializing, even though they are often well prepared academically. It is reasonable to want deaf children to socialize with nonhandicapped children, since that will be their world when they grow up. But mainstreaming can harm some deaf children by separating them from other children like themselves and hindering their acquisition of the communication and social skills necessary for interacting with the deaf community. Deaf children have many opportunities to socialize with nonhandicapped children outside the classroom. There is a concern that mainstreamed students will become isolated and lacking in self-esteem, that they will lapse into passive isolation. The concern is compounded by the realization that mainstreamed programs rarely offer deaf children exposure to deaf adult role models.

A mainstreamed placement requires three conditions to succeed: (1) a critical mass of age and language peers, in other words, enough similar children to constitute a community; (2) staff who can communicate directly, appropriately, and at an adult level with the deaf students; and (3) appropriate and accessible curricula, programs, and services, along with staff knowledgeable about deafness. Since each deaf child responds differently to different settings, based on individual needs and personality, mainstreaming is not always the best option.

The Commission on Education of the Deaf published a report in 1988 that suggested the kinds of factors a school needs to consider when placing deaf children. First, the school must recognize that the communication needs of children vary widely and require careful examination. A key factor here is to determine each deaf child's primary means of communication (American Sign Language, for example) and also the secondary means; in other words, it is necessary to take into account the child's linguistic needs. An assessment of the child's degree of hearing loss is another factor, along with how the child uses any residual hearing that may exist. Program level is an important factor in placement, because deaf children will not do well in programs that are too advanced or, for that matter, not advanced enough.

The concerns about program level and the need to assess language skills both come into play in the next major factor, interaction with peers. Peer relations are important to all children for the growth of personal identity and self-esteem. To interact well with peers means to communicate with them, which requires both language skills and classmates of the right social and intellectual age. The development of a strong identity requires the appropriate role models, not only among peers but among adults, especially deaf peers and adults.

The next factor is the importance of parents' accepting the child's own opinions and preferences when they make their placement decision. After all, it is the child whose interests are at stake and who will participate in the classes and programs. The two related factors of emotional need and motivation also need careful attention. Emotional stability and maturity, which develop unevenly in children and can pose major problems, are often especially high hurdles for deaf children, who must cope with complicated peer relations and the effects of social isolation in many public settings. It is therefore important to evaluate both the school and home environments when considering placement. It is also important to try to determine the child's own aspirations when considering placement, and to give them serious attention.

The two final factors raised by the commissioners are cultural needs and family support. Deaf children, like all young people, come from a variety of cultural backgrounds, but there is a tendency among schools to treat them alike, apparently without realizing the serious learning problems that can arise when children of differing backgrounds are made to fit a common mold. One potential support for a deaf child in such a situation is, of course, the family, which must provide a secure foundation for the child's emotional and intellectual maturation. Deaf children, like all children, benefit from a supportive family.

I applaud the report of the commissioners and would add another point. Deaf children have the right to be deaf and to have their own language and culture. We must enrich their lives with respect and a positive attitude toward their language and culture. To place them in an environment where they cannot communicate is unconstitutional and, in a way, a form of abuse. A better future for the deaf children of this generation and for the next generation means we must always remembers the child's right to be deaf and to respect and dignity. We, as teachers in both regular and special education, play a crucial role through our responsibility for what occurs in the classroom from hour to hour and day to day. We provide a wide variety of learning opportunities and instructional styles, often above and beyond what the curriculum dictates. We are held accountable for our performance, and we are personally and professionally committed to providing an appropriate learning environment for each deaf child.

References

Commission on Education of the Deaf. *Toward Equality*. Washington, D.C.: Government Printing Office, 1988. Pp. 22–23.

Stewart, Larry G. "The Education of Deaf Children Is a Process—Not Just a Placement," Proceedings from the conference "Reclaiming the Future: Life after LRE." In *Reclaiming the Future,* ed. D. M. Denton, p. 117. Frederick, Md.: Maryland School for the Deaf, 1990.

The Education of Deaf Children in France

ANNETTE GOROUBEN

In France, we hear so many conflicting accounts about the education of the deaf in the United States. Idealized by those who know only Gallaudet University, the United States has taken on mythic proportions: across the Atlantic they do it much better than we do. Others reply that Gallaudet is not the United States and that much controversy remains over methods and aims. To assist in the task of comparison, I will survey what happens in France to children up to age six—nursery and preschool age. I base my discussion on an analysis of data drawn from a questionnaire that I sent to all the schools and centers in France that accept deaf children. The one hundred schools that responded, or 80 percent of the institutions that received questionnaires, provide a truly representative sample.

Schools and Centers Sampled

All the schools and centers are supported by federal funds, from Social Security alone or in conjunction with other agencies, and they charge no fee to families. The state also pays 80 percent of transportation expenses. The centers (see Table 1) have a common denominator: the staff consists mainly of physicians (otolaryngologists, pediatricians, child psychiatrists), paramedical personnel (speech therapists,

Annette Gorouben is director of the Experimental Bilingual Center for Deaf Children (Centre Bilingue pour Enfants Sourds).

Table 1   Types of Centers and Schools Surveyed

CAMSPS (Medico-Social Centers of Preschool Action)	35
Monovalent	12
Polyvalent	23
SSESAD (Treatment Service and Special Education at Home)	32
Hospital audiology departments	9
Public schools (mainstream and annex classes)	9
INJS (National Institutes for the Young Deaf)	4
Other (including one specialized nursery)	10

psychomotor therapists), teachers , *educateurs* trained in special education, and social workers. *Educateurs* function almost as regular teachers, especially for younger children; they are trained in a three-year university program. Thirty-three of the centers have deaf educational personnel, whose job titles are hard to specify, except for the few who have received their special *educateur* degree.

Preschool education for deaf children began in France, as in other countries, during the early 1970s, with the appearance of early diagnosis and the miniaturization of hearing aids. The Medico-Social Centers of Preschool Action (CAMSPs) were created between 1979 and 1981. CAMSPs can be monovalent, accepting only children who are deaf, or polyvalent, accepting children with all kinds of handicaps and problems (intellectual, motor, sensory). Our survey dealt solely with monovalent centers, which account for about 34 percent of all the CAMSPs. The polyvalent centers accept, on average, six deaf children, who may or may not have other disabilities.

Table 2 presents breakdowns of the ages at which children are admitted. Very early intervention, that is, before the second year of life, is rare. The most common ages at admission are one to one and one-half years (18 percent) and two years (28 percent). Only 8 percent of the children are under age one and 16 percent are between ages two and three. The large proportion of older childen in the centers is a function not of the time of diagnosis but of the services offered by the schools, which begin seeing children at nursery school age (around three years old).

Table 2   Average Age of Admission to Centers and Schools
(100 Institutions Responding)

Age	No. of Children	Percentage
0–0.5 years	1	1
0.5–1.0 years	7	7
1.0–1.5 years	18	18
1.5–2.0 years	28	28
2.0–2.5 years	7	7
2.5–3.0 years	9	9
3.0–3.5 years	3	3
3.5–4.0 years	8	8
4.0–4.5 years	5	5
4.5–5.0 years	4	4
5.0–5.5 years	2	2
5.5–6.0 years	8	8

Parental Participation

Eighty percent of the centers and schools indicate they have programs for parents: interviews with the psychologist or social worker; parent groups led by the most appropriate staff person (psychiatrist or psychologist); or group sessions with staff. There is a general awareness of the difficulties that hearing parents, and even deaf parents, encounter immediately after the diagnosis of deafness. The institutions that do not provide programs for parents are generally schools or hospital auditory centers that have no statutory provision for such services.

In general, parents are very involved, especially mothers. Most fathers (82 percent) come to the centers from time to time, but in general they find it harder than their wives to get personally involved in the education of younger children, and they also may find it more difficult to express, through involvement at the centers, the pain they feel at the child's disability. Most parents participate through speech therapy sessions with their child, but some also join in sessions of French Sign Language (LSF).

The important role of women in the work force means that children are frequently placed in nursery schools. Since virtually all nursery school staff are hearing persons, nearly all deaf children have experience with a hearing environment by the time they reach kindergarten. All the centers surveyed reported frequent contacts with schools that accept mainstreamed children.

Methods

Within the general consensus about the need to give very young children early access to communication, there remains much dispute among professionals, and hence among parents, about the best means. Should the deaf child's first language be LSF? Should the child use it exclusively or in conjunction with other language modes like cued speech? Should we give priority to the parents' language and add manual communication later?

It is widely accepted that the parents must make the final choice in these decisions, though we know how difficult the choice is. The parents of a child just diagnosed as deaf are in a very emotional state and lack firsthand experience with the methods we are proposing to them. More often it is the first professional the parents encounter at the moment of diagnosis who most influences their choice.

The extreme variety of language modes uncovered by the survey surprised us. Counting the different techniques and communication modes, we identified twenty-five different combinations of LSF, cued speech, signed French, the verbo-tonal method, and Borel-Maisonny's gestures, or "cues." (The verbo-tonal method, created in Yugoslavia, uses musical and body-movement rhythms and special equipment for teaching speech and voice training; the Borel-Maisonny gestures are hand movements designed to encourage kinesthetic perceptions of phonemes.) We grouped the combinations into two basic groups, pure oralist and bilingual. The pure oralist option includes four variants:

1. Pure oral (lipreading, auditory training, and speech), in nine centers
2. Oral + cued speech, in seven centers
3. Oral + cued speech + verbo-tonal, in ten centers
4. Oral + cued speech + signed French, in twenty-seven centers

The bilingual option includes two variants:

1. Combinations of LSF and cued speech, in twenty-eight centers
2. LSF + oral, sometimes associated with signed French and verbo-tonal, in twelve centers

Cued speech is fairly easy to institute in the centers, but there is a financial problem in the hiring of the "coders." More important, parents participated in cued speech only to a limited degree: of the seventy-two centers that said they used cued speech, parents practiced it in 51 percent. The use of cues greatly slows the pace of speech, and in addition we cannot assume that all adults have a good phonological knowledge of their own language. Signed French is taught by hearing staff in thirteen centers that favor the oralist position, usually in association with cued speech.

Forty of the centers teach LSF, and at twenty-three other centers parents must find LSF instruction outside the institution. The bilingual approach assumes that most deaf children have hearing parents, yet it is often hard to persuade hearing parents (and sometimes deaf parents) to sign with their young children. More than half of the parents surveyed did not learn LSF. When highly motivated parents master LSF and use it in exchanges at home, the children more easily acquire LSF themselves. The centers that provide LSF instruction do so in ways that limit what the children can learn. At the thirty-three centers that employ deaf staff members, the survey responses indicate that only sixteen staffers have adequate contact with the children; the others can spend only about an hour a week per student on LSF, which is not really enough to provide proper instruction.

The uneven teaching of LSF at the surveyed schools and centers touches an issue raised in recent federal laws that give parents the option of choosing either an oralist or bilingual education for their deaf child. The problem is that high-quality bilingualism requires that the child learn LSF as soon as possible, to permit the development of intellectual powers, of information acquisition, of expressive abilities, and of emotional growth. Bilingualism also means that children must have good auditory training early in life, during important formative periods, and that they should encounter the written language very early, as happens to hearing children in everyday life, in order to understand its function and to learn the pleasure of books. The survey data suggest that the schools and centers remain far from achieving these ideals.

Implementation of Methods

If the philosophy of a center usually depends on the sensibilities of its staff, its methods often depend on the local situation: teacher training, the availability of competent deaf people, and the availability of potential employees. In France, staff who work with young deaf children do not mandatorily receive the same practical training. In Paris, for example, speech therapists get very little exposure to sign language; for more complete training they must attend additional workshops, for which their center cannot always pay, whether it be for techniques designed to facilitate the teaching of speech (like the verbo-tonal method or cued speech) or for communication skills in sign language. Those deaf persons who have not passed their *baccalaureat* test to enter the university and obtain the *educateur* degree in special education have no program comprehensive enough to train them to work with young deaf children and their hearing parents. The difficulties they encounter when they are hired for teaching teams, where the hearing teachers may or may not sign, where they often feel isolated, and where they are asked to do a job for which they are not prepared, can be discouraging and cause tension among the staff. Such training, which we have been demanding for years, should be organized immediately if we want high-quality bilingualism.

Conclusion

While deaf people have evolved a visual culture of their own, worthy of respect, they should never be excluded to access from the general cultural, economic, and political heritage of their country. The cornerstone of this access is the early use of a language, which permits the interchange and open-mindedness that is necessary for deaf and hearing people to live together satisfactorily. The stakes are very high for our deaf children, who will develop their personalities and knowledge of the world only through proper education.

Preschool and Early Intervention in the United States

RACHEL STONE

The educational system in the United States for all children extends from first through twelfth grades. Kindergarten for five-year-olds is mandated in some states and optional in others. Preschool education involves children ages three to five, and early intervention programs involve children through the age of two. Although preschool education is optional in most states, many state programs for the deaf have offered preschool programs for the past twenty to twenty-five years.

Public Laws 94-142 and 99-457

In 1975, the U.S. Congress passed the Education for All Handicapped Children Act, which went into effect in October of 1977. This law, Public Law 94-142, mandated a free and appropriate public education for all handicapped children ages three through twenty-one, with flexibility where state laws were inconsistent allowing for a beginning age range of three through five and ending with ages ranging from nineteen to twenty-one.

In 1986, when PL 94-142 was renewed, an amendment, PL 99-457, mandated preschool education. The new law puts education for infants through the age of two at the states' discretion but makes education for children three through five years old mandatory on a

---

Rachel Stone is principal and assistant superintendent of education at the Indiana School for the Deaf.

statewide basis if a state wants to receive federal funding for pre-school education. By the 1990–1991 school year, states were required to assure the federal government that they were providing programs for children three through five years old, or they would lose any federal funding for preschool programs they might have received under former grant awards.

The Commission on Education of the Deaf, appointed in 1987 and charged with studying the educational system for deaf children in the United States, presented its report, "Toward Equality: The Education of the Deaf," to President Reagan in 1988. In that report, the commission found that the education received by deaf students nationally was not equal to the education received by their hearing peers. In spite of the new methods used in past years to educate the deaf, the average reading skill of deaf adults on a national scale remained the equivalent of a third- or fourth-grade reading level.

The commission recommended that the federal government require states to promote early identification of deaf infants through the use of screening procedures to detect hearing loss. The government should "require state educational agencies to conduct statewide planning and implementation activities in compliance with PL 99-457, including the establishment of programs and personnel standards, which specifically address the educational and psychological needs of families with young children who are deaf." The report urged that persons working with young deaf children and their families "should be professionally trained in the area of deafness and early intervention to serve this population" (Commission 1988, p. 8).

Deaf Children in Preschool and Early Intervention Programs

Early-intervention programs in the United States are the responsibility of the individual state. Many programs are established on a statewide basis through state schools for the deaf or through private or public agencies.

In March 1991, the Indiana School for the Deaf contacted and surveyed eight schools to gather information on early intervention and preschool programming (list appended). Most of the schools had in-home services as well as center-based residential and day programs. Most of them were either residential or day programs serving only the deaf population. The survey did not include school systems with a few deaf children who were being mainstreamed with the hearing population.

The schools surveyed employed part-time parent advisers and full-time teachers and aides for 216 deaf children in early-intervention programs. Of these teachers and aides, only two were deaf. In the preschool programs, most of the teachers and aides were hearing; only five were deaf, and they worked with a total of 259 deaf children. Hearing people administered all programs but one. Many administrators expressed the desire to have more deaf professionals in the programs; my assumption is that teacher-training programs historically have not attracted deaf applicants for early childhood education.

A standard format for providing early intervention is used across the United States. A professional trained to work with parents and families visits the home once a week, to work with the parents, primarily mothers, in the areas of communication, language development, auditory training, and the care and use of hearing aids. This format enables the professional to give important information about deafness, listen to the parents' concerns, and assist in dealing with the variety of problems they may encounter. Many programs provide hearing parents the opportunity to interact with deaf adults on a social level or through parent-to-parent contact. Information about the deaf community is shared with hearing parents, and they are encouraged to participate in activities of the deaf community. Most preschool teachers agree that children entering preschool who have had the benefit of any early-intervention program have more advanced skills than those who have not. These children demonstrate fewer behavior problems, more emotional maturity, and advanced language and communication skills.

Most preschool programs use manually coded signs representing the English language. They also offer speech and auditory training. A few adopt American Sign Language (ASL) as the language of instruction. However, finding quality ASL classes and getting parents to attend are two of the major problems facing educators of the deaf.

Most educators agree that young children need interaction with peers and adults willing to communicate with them to develop effective communication. All agree that the adults in the environment need to be responsive and willing to communicate by any means.

When the family has completed the program or when the child is old enough, he or she usually attends a center-based preschool program. Again, most professionals in these center-based programs are hearing, with a few programs employing teachers and aides who are deaf. Often social services are provided on a limited basis in connection with the program. Parent support groups proliferate, and audiological services are usually provided. Occasionally there is access to family or individual counseling. Although many of the programs I surveyed support team teaching and have used it at one time or another, few used it consistently. However, many were discussing it, and one program was planning a team approach using one deaf and one hearing teacher for each classroom.

Bilingual/Bicultural Education

In January 1990, the Indiana School for the Deaf (ISD) adopted a bilingual/bicultural (BiBi) philosophy of education. One of two schools in the nation adopting the BiBi approach, ISD believes that it is imperative to have deaf role models and native users of American Sign Language in the educational environment. The bilingual and bicultural philosophy and approach involve teaching two separate and distinct languages, American Sign Language and English, as well as teaching two distinct cultures, deaf and hearing. The language of instruction in the classroom is American Sign Language. Students study ASL as their hearing counterparts in the public schools study English. English is taught to deaf students as a second language primarily through reading and writing. For those with the ability to learn spoken English, a functional approach is employed rather than traditional methods.

During the 1990–1991 school year, much experimentation occurred in ISD's classrooms. Three deaf classroom teachers, one deaf physical education teacher, and one deaf aide were assigned to the preschool department to work with nursery school children. Videotaping of deaf and hearing teachers in other departments provided a way of comparing teaching strategies. Students were exposed to ASL in a variety of ways, such as presentations by deaf storytellers in the classrooms of hearing teachers and the showing of videotapes featuring deaf signers of ASL. Deaf and hearing teachers sometimes combined their classes for specific activities, thus demonstrating both deaf and hearing role models.

Team teaching was emphasized during the 1991–1992 school year. Team teaching can provide a school environment that focuses on the educational development of deaf children by exposing them to American Sign Language and English, as well as the cultures of deaf and hearing people. It means that classes with deaf and hearing teachers are often combined for instruction and mutual learning, a strategy being developed on an ongoing basis.

The Indiana School for the Deaf also identified a variety of new staff positions in 1991–1992 that would continue the process of creating a bilingual and bicultural educational environment. Most of these positions were implemented for the 1992–1993 school year. They include ASL instructors to teach students and staff; two coordinators of American Sign Language/English as a second language (ASL/ESL), who are responsible for methodology and strategies for using and teaching the two languages; a Deaf Studies coordinator to develop a curriculum on the history, literature, and culture of the deaf for all grade levels; and a coordinator for orientation and transition to plan programming for students who transfer from schools where ASL and the bilingual/bicultural approach have not been used. In-service programs train and inform staff of developments in all of these areas.

Conclusion

Young children need a psychologically safe, language-enriched environment in which to learn. Children need acceptance for who they are linguistically, culturally, and developmentally to become responsive adults. The goals of the bilingual/bicultural philosophy coincide with all goals set for deaf students: to promote identity and build positive self-esteem, and to provide deaf students with the opportunity to develop and maximize their potential.

These goals will be accomplished by providing ample educational programs and opportunities in an environment rich with appropriate role models, where deaf and hearing professionals operate on a level of mutual trust and respect, and where opportunities for the advancement of deaf people are promoted.

References

Commission on Education of the Deaf. *Toward Equality: The Education of the Deaf. A Report to the President and the Congress of the United States.* Washington, D.C.: Government Printing Office, 1988.

Public Law 94-142. Code of Federal Regulations, Federal Register, National Archives and Records Service, General Services Administration. (Special Edition of the Federal Register). Washington, D.C.: Government Printing Office, revised July 1, 1984.

Public Law 99-457, The Education of the Handicapped Act: Amendment of 1986. Disseminated by the National Association of State Directors of Special Education, November 1986.

List of Schools Surveyed

American School for the Deaf, Hartford, Conn.: preschool

Arizona School for the Deaf, Phoenix, Ariz.: early intervention and preschool

Arizona School for the Deaf, Tucson, Ariz.: early intervention

Florida School for the Deaf and Blind, St. Augustine, Fla.: preschool

Indiana School for the Deaf, Indianapolis, Ind.: early intervention and preschool

Kentucky School for the Deaf, Danville, Ky.: early intervention and preschool

The Learning Center, Framingham, Mass.: early intervention

Maryland School for the Deaf, Frederick and Columbia, Md.: preschool

The Spirit of BiBi:
Two Languages and Two Cultures

DAVID O. REYNOLDS

What Does BiBi Mean?

The bilingual/bicultural philosophy (BiBi) sets new, high expectations for deaf children. It promotes fluency in two languages—American Sign Language (ASL) and English—by creating an environment where deaf people are recognized as members of a distinct cultural and linguistic minority group.

BiBi is for all children who are hard of hearing as well as those who are profoundly deaf. Each of these individuals requires a visual language to fully develop their communicative potential as human beings. ASL is the only true language of deaf people in the United States and Canada. It meets all the requirements of linguistic analysis including grammar, syntax, and semantics. It has its own vocabulary, which includes loan signs borrowed from English—just as all languages add lexical items (words or signs) by borrowing from languages they come into contact with. The analytical proof of ASL's legitimacy and effectiveness as a language is overwhelming.

The first step in initiating BiBi is to involve deaf people. This one detail distinguishes the BiBi philosophy from every other methodology of educating deaf people that has sprouted up in the last 150 years. Until now, every technique, every strategy for teaching deaf people has come from the minds of hearing people who believed that the goal of educating deaf people was to make them just like hearing

David O. Reynolds is bilingual/bicultural coordinator at the Indiana School for the Deaf.

people—to make them not deaf! BiBi was created by deaf people. BiBi will be led by deaf people. If it is not, then it is not truly BiBi.

Hearing people have a place in this philosophy as allies. The concept of being an ally implies "equal partner"—not above, not below, but on the same level: peer. Building an alliance is difficult, serious work. An alliance is more than a coalition of diverse groups with various interests who join forces to pursue a common goal. An alliance requires trust and commitment to the full agenda of all parties involved. Allies work with—not for—each other, and have respect for both cultures.

BiBi means that the whole school changes. Hearing people must change their attitudes: how they perceive deaf people. They must shift their perspective from a medical/pathological view to a cultural view. They must understand the self-definition of deaf people as a cultural and linguistic minority group: they are not broken, not handicapped, not second-class citizens, but members of a people with a unique language and culture. This change will promote an environment where deaf and hearing can work together as equals.

Deaf people must throw away the fear of challenging the system. We must stop saying "Be careful" as an excuse for inaction. We must abandon the role of the oppressed, stop accepting whatever the oppressor chooses to give us, and begin to take bold, active steps to improve not only the educational system but our entire cultural status.

We must change the process. Attitudes do not change quickly or easily. Discussion, dialogue, and mediation are vital. Conflicts and misperceptions are common and must be handled carefully and with great respect for each individual involved. Through this process, people will develop awareness, sensitivity, and respect for each other's differences. Slowly, a foundation of trust will evolve.

Empowerment is the core of the BiBi philosophy. It is a process of identifying and dismantling oppression. It involves describing the smallest, seemingly insignificant details of the relationship between the oppressor and the oppressed. It requires exposing the emotions and becoming vulnerable to each other. The end result will free both deaf and hearing people from oppression and give birth to a new partnership in the education of deaf children.

Changing the Deaf Education System

Unfortunately, there is no nice, simple procedure with easy directions to follow to create this kind of change. In 1990, after four years of discussion, the administration at the Indiana School for the Deaf (ISD) agreed to commit to a new mission statement and philosophy. Hearing and deaf people at ISD implemented a fifteen-year plan to make the transition to bilingual/bicultural education.

This change generated more discussion. Educators, parents, linguists, whole communities, and many others who are interested or involved with deaf education entered into dialogue with us. Most of them had their own interpretation of what BiBi means. They speculated that it was (1) a methodology using ASL in the classroom; (2) the offering of Deaf Studies courses to students; (3) the elimination of English; (4) the elimination of speech training; or (5) the departure of all hearing people from schools for the deaf, giving deaf people full ownership and control.

None of these definitions is correct. BiBi is much more than just a curriculum, and it contains no strategy to get rid of hearing people!

Another misconception is that schools that have a multicultural philosophy are a step ahead. In fact, they have bypassed a critical phase. By leaping into multiculturalism, they have ignored the dominant, oppressive dynamic in the system—that between deaf and hearing people. BiBi must occur first, or the multicultural emphasis will only enforce the prejudice that deaf people have no unique culture of their own.

BiBi is not an end product. It is a transitional phase on the road to true multiculturalism. Just as you cannot start a BiBi philosophy without deaf people, you cannot start a multicultural philosophy without recognizing and accepting deaf culture—which means dealing with the last 150 years of attempted cultural genocide.

Our definition of BiBi has grown out of all of these discussions, as we have confronted and refuted the mistaken ideas of so many people. We had to begin teaching virtually everyone, including professionals and lay people, the real meaning of BiBi.

BiBi simply means learning two languages and two cultures. It means recognizing the similarities and respecting the differences between the two. BiBi does involve changes in the curriculum and management of schools for the deaf. It does use ASL as the language of instruction in all classrooms. English is taught as a second language—with an emphasis on reading, writing, and translation. BiBi does take steps to place deaf people in decision-making positions within the school administration.

The most critical part of implementing BiBi is that deaf people must be involved in all stages and at all levels. Strong, empowered deaf leadership is vital. Actually putting a BiBi philosophy in place requires the concurrent redesign and development of several components. Specific areas include, but may not be limited to, the following:

1. Employment. Work within and recruit from the state systems for teacher certification and hiring. There are many deaf professionals out there, we just need to let them know that the opportunities exist. Under the employment rubric we include activities and issues like procedures for recruiting teachers, administrative and dormitory staff, interpreters, and others; criteria and procedures for screening; guidelines for interviews; and criteria and processes for hiring.

2. Evaluation of students. BiBi uses a "whole child" perspective. It focuses on the needs of the child not only from an academic view but also from the perspectives of socialization and emotional well-being. In the audiology clinic, BiBi emphasizes a functional approach. It also stresses language-skills assessment for appropriate placement in communication development programs. After-school programs are critical for cultural transmission to occur. It is outside of the classroom that young deaf people learn the ways of their culture, of their own people. Peer interaction develops the self-esteem, confidence, pride, and sense of belonging necessary for successful interaction in the world. The presence of deaf role models promotes goal setting and expectations for high achievement.

3. Curriculum. The emphasis here is on the process, not the product. Each school must develop its own set of principles and

leadership guidelines and start to practice them. During this process, a product will grow—a curriculum. All the components come together here as individual people grow and change through their participation in the process. Empowerment manifests itself as the alliance becomes real.

BiBi throws away the traditional model of imposing a product on a system that people have had no role in developing: Product → Process. This model forces discussion because people resist changes that they were not consulted about.

The BiBi model reverses this by involving people in the process of planning the change: Process → Product. This gives people a sense of ownership and responsibility that is lacking in the traditional model. The investment creates a desire to translate the theory from the drawing board into reality. The beauty of BiBi is that once you commit to the process you begin to experience the transformation with other committed individuals, and the product becomes real right before your eyes. You have a "living" curriculum.

Implementation of the process of creating a living curriculum should include: (a) development and design; (b) a consistent and complementary program through all age and grade levels; (c) deaf cultural perspectives included in all subject areas; (d) attention to content areas such as ASL grammar, English as a second language, deaf culture, and Deaf Studies.

4. Parental involvement. Parents must be consultants in the process of educating their children. Two ways of accomplishing that are through ASL classes and support groups.

5. Speech/communication center. Develop a communication center that facilitates pragmatic communication skills through a variety of languages and modalities, including speaking, reading/writing, and signing. Use a functional approach. Separate spoken English from regular classes. Distinguish between speech and language. Teach English as a second language. Emphasize that the ability to speak English is a skill or craft, and that those students who are unable to master it should not feel inferior.

6. Staff development. Participatory management revolutionizes the top-to-bottom hierarchical chain of command. The practice of "teaming," a deaf cultural strength as opposed to the hearing culture's emphasis on individualism, involves everyone by giving them responsibility and therefore a sense of ownership.

Learning to Work Together

In addition to the task-oriented processes of implementation is the personal development of each individual as he or she recognizes and responds to the forces of change. A bilingual/bicultural approach to the education of deaf children is a direct attack against oppression, and therefore has ramifications for members of both sides of the dichotomy.

People have strong reactions to being identified as either oppressed or as oppressor. They do not like it, and usually deny it vigorously. But this relationship of oppression is precisely what perpetuates the current ineffectual and repressive system of deaf education. Traditionally we have ignored it, made fun of it, and acted as if it did not exist. BiBi identifies it as the enemy that it really is.

People feel threatened when oppression is identified in this way. Over the course of our lives, each of us has learned how to handle it in our own peculiar way, and, quite frankly, most of us have developed a level of comfort with our own role. A challenge to this comfort is disturbing, and people react in a variety of ways. Some rise to the occasion, feeling enlightened and accepting it as positive feedback that promotes personal and collective growth; others, feeling attacked or persecuted, hide by becoming angry. Almost everyone feels some fear, and guilt and shame are also common.

Dealing with the volatility of already fragile relationships is the greatest challenge of implementing a bilingual/bicultural philosophy. Overcoming these barriers requires a three-step offensive.

In the first step, dialogue, we emphasize the process, not the product. We accept that it will take time and patience. We listen to each other. We discuss, and discuss, and discuss. We use third-party mediation to resolve conflicts and perceptions. And finally, we believe that people can change through good processes.

In the second step, results, we seek mutual respect for each other's culture and language, and freedom from previous roles as oppressor and oppressed. We cultivate increased sensitivity, respect, and trust, with the hope of becoming true allies. Our goals are empowerment as individuals and equal partners, and recognition of deaf people as members of a cultural minority group.

The third step, facilitation, calls for the balanced participation of deaf and hearing members on every team. We create new positions on the administrative team for two BiBi coordinators. The two coordinators will oversee the entire implementation process and perform several other important functions. They will implement an aggressive public relations campaign, with deaf people playing an important, visible role, to overcome the "wait and see" attitude that has historically afflicted deaf schools and contributed to their image as a "last resort" by many parents and professionals. The coordinators will also guide participants through the process of change, which will include mediating cultural conflicts and misunderstandings, monitoring the whole school to keep each component aligned, and serving as liaison between the deaf community, parents, and the school. The coordinators will work for parallel reform outside the school, in the state, and nationally, and will serve as a resource for other deaf schools and assist them in their progress toward BiBi.

Understanding the True Spirit of BiBi

The true spirit of BiBi will be reflected not only in tangible improvements in education and quality of services but also in the nature of deaf and hearing relationships. The BiBi philosophy will take root in each individual and grow into the strong bond of equals joined in a common struggle.

BiBi signifies a cultural revolution. To be effective, BiBi must be expanded beyond the setting of the residential school to all systems and programs that interact with our schools on any level. In deaf-education training programs, we must shift from the pathological to the cultural view of deafness. We must require language proficiency in ASL, and we must redesign certification requirements—both state and national—and testing procedures. Currently tests are administered in the deaf person's second language, English. Scores will therefore more likely reflect English-language proficiency, not a person's knowledge and skill as a teacher. These tests contain items that are appropriate for members of the hearing culture, such as questions about music, but contain an inherent bias against deaf applicants. It is necessary to redesign the tests from a deaf cultural perspective and administer them in American Sign Language. In interpreter-training programs, we must emphasize ASL. We must retrain people in the nature of interpretation—what it is and how to do it. How can we mediate between two languages in culturally appropriate ways?

We must amend state and national laws to require that hospitals identify deaf babies and refer their families to the deaf community and the state school for the deaf. This is important for two reasons. First, most parents of children born deaf or hard of hearing have never met a deaf adult. Personal contact with a deaf adult as soon as possible will ease the parents' grieving process as they begin to understand that there is hope for their child to live a full life in which he or she can excel. Second, the critical-age hypothesis suggests that language must be acquired by the age of six for a human being to develop full communicative capacity. This means that early exposure to a visual language such as ASL is imperative.

We must transfer deaf children from special education programs, because they have unique needs that are not being met by programs designed for the disabled. The deaf school offers transitional orientation programs for those who enter late. These programs are designed to facilitate late language acquisition and teach basic cultural rules.

We must redesign the federal Deaf Education Act of 1986. This is another piece of legislation that was crafted without sufficient participation by deaf people, and currently applies to only three types of schools. It comes from a medical perspective and does not recognize the cultural and linguistic minority status of deaf people. We need to transfer the responsibility and accountability of deaf education out of special education and under a new Deaf Education Act that emphasizes BiBi. We must avoid being subsumed under the Bilingual Education Act, because the goal of that legislation is the elimination of native languages.

BiBi is not just a new fad in the checkered history of deaf education. It is different because it is a deaf-developed program. A century and a half during which hearing people dictated how to educate members of the deaf community is coming to an end.

BiBi is the practical and political answer to mainstreaming that will ensure the survival of residential schools for the deaf. As we expand and improve the services we have to offer deaf children, enrollment will begin to rise. As we confront and dismantle the myths about our culture and our language, enrollment will continue to increase. As we prove the success of BiBi with higher academic test scores in all areas, parents will begin to choose residential schools as their first choice when it comes to deciding what is best for their deaf child. They will choose BiBi not only because it works, but because their perception of the schools will change. It is our goal that parents see and understand that residential schools for the deaf are like private boarding schools that bestow honor and prestige on all who attend.

BiBi will distinguish us clearly from mainstreaming and therefore guarantee the survival of our schools. Deaf culture and language are taught through the residential schools. If the schools are eliminated, so is our culture—we lose the ability to transmit our history, our language, and our heritage. This makes BiBi a potent political issue that requires political action.

BiBi means personal and cultural empowerment for deaf people. It signals the end of oppression, if we have the courage to achieve it. Although BiBi will affect the entire culture of deaf people and the larger culture of the United States, the bottom line is that BiBi begins in each of us. The BiBi philosophy is a revolutionary strategy that has come from the minds and souls of deaf people. Deaf people will lead this movement for change. We will reclaim our language and our culture, and we will save our schools.

The school for the deaf has been, and will always be, home base for the deaf community. It is the heart and soul of deaf culture. By establishing high expectations for deaf youth and providing them with the tools to meet those expectations, the residential school for the deaf will become recognized in the wider hearing world as the core that it is. The school will then become a resource for the development of centralized mainstream programs in large cities that can offer day/residential programs and still have the full benefit of being a BiBi program. Again, the key is that deaf people participate fully in the entire process of planning and implementation, as well as having ongoing responsibilities for monitoring and consulting. This means deaf people must be on staff.

An outgrowth of BiBi will be greater involvement of the deaf community at large with the deaf schools and the education of deaf children. This will help deaf youths form a positive identity as they come into contact with many deaf adults who are successful in a wide variety of fields. The impact of role models cannot be underestimated.

BiBi means "the big picture." It means the overhaul of the entire system of education for deaf people in America (and internationally as well). It means the rupture of the old, familiar relationship between the oppressor and the oppressed and the creation of new, healthy alliances with hearing people who understand and respect deaf culture. We must take the initiative and lead the charge for change! We have nothing to lose and everything to gain. We can put an end to the last 150 years of damage to deaf children.

Working toward BiBi is not just a job. It requires a deep commitment, the willingness to allow yourself to change, to feel vulnerable, and yet to find within yourself the courage and conviction to continue to work for the future of all deaf children regardless of audiological measurement of hearing loss.

BiBi means cultural survival. It means that deaf people are recognized as truly equal, not looked down on and scorned, but seen as unique and valuable. BiBi means that we, the deaf, will get our language and culture back; and for the first time in history we will have our rights.

"Signing Naturally": An American Sign Language Curriculum

ELLA MAE LENTZ

This paper outlines the development of *Signing Naturally, An American Sign Language (ASL) Curriculum*. This curriculum encourages students to develop communicative competence and cultural awareness in a classroom environment that allows for natural language learning.

Why Develop an ASL Curriculum?

The 1970s and '80s saw the passage of several significant federal laws and regulations that increased the demands of deaf people for accessibility, including the use of interpreters. In addition, the American public was encountering sign language more often in the theater, at movies, and on television programs. Research about American Sign Language (ASL) was piquing the curiosity of academics and other experts, who began investigating the language's structure and the culture of its users. The deaf community was demanding service providers more qualified in their sign language skills and appropriate cross-cultural behaviors, and they sought acceptance of ASL courses as satisfying requirements toward school and college graduation, foreign language proficiency, and humanities courses. The result was an increased demand for quality instruction in American Sign Language.

Ella Mae Lentz is an American Sign Language instructor at Vista College in Berkeley, California.

It is estimated that in California alone, over 10,000 students enroll in sign language courses each year.

Although ASL is well over 200 years old and is America's fourth most commonly used language, only recently has it been taught in schools and colleges. There is a dearth of instructional materials, and experts have not yet analyzed the new linguistic research for its applications to teaching ASL in the classroom. Opportunities for formal academic study in the instruction of ASL have been limited. Often ASL teachers were selected for their language fluency rather than their background in language teaching. These teachers relied heavily on student textbooks or tried to develop their own instructional materials. There were no overall curricular materials to help teachers establish a cultural context for language instruction, make decisions about how to sequence course materials, and develop activities that allowed students to progress from one-word responses to the spontaneous expression of thoughts and feelings on a discourse level.

The ASL textbooks were excellent—as far as they went. One was organized according to grammatical points. From our experience, this is not the most effective way to design a language course, because even though students may master grammatical structures, they will not learn natural conversational skills. Another textbook was organized according to culturally relevant topics accompanied by supplemental grammatical points. It dealt with language on a discourse level using videotapes of native signers in actual conversations. However, the videotapes sometimes incorporated complex grammar and advanced vocabulary, and there were often gaps between what was expressed on the tape and what students could comprehend.

These texts did not provide a natural basis for language learning. Children, and second-language learners, learn language in a social context, in the target language, building their vocabulary on the basis of the here and now. They learn concrete words before abstract ones. They learn by interacting with a person who introduces new words and patterns, showing how to convey something in a particular situation for a particular purpose.

How Did We Get Started?

In 1984, three of us in the American Sign Language Department at Vista College—Cheri Smith, Ken Mikos, and I—received funds from the U.S. Department of Education Fund for the Improvement of Postsecondary Education for a three-year project to develop the curriculum, to provide a mechanism for communication and interchange among ASL programs around the country, and to provide a basis for uniform training and certification programs. Our target population was postsecondary students, especially those at Vista College. Their average age was twenty-three to fifty, and many already had college degrees and jobs. Some took ASL courses because they wanted to learn a beautiful and fun language, and because the users live right here in the United States, all around them. Some had, or wanted to attract, deaf customers or employees; others hoped to become interpreters; still others were artists who wanted to see if they could incorporate ASL into their work. Some simply had deaf relatives or neighbors.

In addition to studying different approaches to second-language teaching, we asked students in our program to describe how they used ASL and to assess whether or not their courses had prepared them to use ASL in real-life situations. We also surveyed members of the deaf community regarding situations and topics of discussion they had with hearing signers.

The surveys and research revealed the need for an approach that emphasized interpersonal communication to help students achieve communicative competence. The functional-notional approach focuses on the "functions" or communicative purposes of everyday interaction. Do you want to introduce people to each other? Do you want to direct someone to do or not to do something? Do you want to talk about a film or something in the room? Do you want to recite a poem?

We decided to teach vocabulary, grammatical structures, and expressions according to their language function; that is, we would use situations predicating everyday deaf-hearing activities and encounters that would give meaning to the function. An indirect benefit to students would be cultural awareness and cross-cultural adjustment skills.

What Is the Structure of the Curriculum?

Since most ASL teachers are not trained specifically as language teachers, we wrote detailed lesson plans that included what to teach and how to teach it. We developed activities and materials (handouts, worksheets, transparencies, and videotapes) to help teachers implement the curriculum. We also developed a student workbook and videotext for supplemental practice outside classroom.

In the classroom, we created a natural language environment by setting up situations that allowed students to concentrate on the purpose rather than the mechanics of conversation. Students build vocabulary starting with what they see in their immediate environment. They learn grammar in the context of the situations they are likely to encounter. More important, the situations teach the distinctive aspects of deaf culture and cross-cultural interaction. The dialogue formats and grammar are reinforced in the student's workbook with demonstrations and through practice on the videotext.

The entire curriculum consists of about 400 hours of instruction, with over twenty-five units, divided into four levels. Each unit focuses on a primary language function with a few other minor functions, and includes four basic activity types: Introduction, Sign Production, Extended Comprehension, and Interaction. The activity types correspond to the natural language-learning process whereby comprehension skills are developed before production skills. Students progress from structured dialogues to spontaneous exchanges. There are also "breakaways" to develop and practice not only numbers but also spatial awareness, fingerspelling, expansion of vocabulary and classifiers, team-building, and facial expressions.

The student workbook and videotext correspond to the curriculum, and they review what is taught in the classroom. Each unit has three basic parts. "Language in Action" provides dialogues in a natural setting that cover the main functions introduced in the curriculum unit. "Grammar Notes and Practice" drills on the main grammatical aspects of the language function(s) of the curriculum unit. "Comprehension" provides a chance to further develop comprehension skills through interactive activities that require the student to perform— by writing, drawing, or circling—what is being shown on the videotape. An answer key in back of the workbook enables the students to check their work. The workbook also contains cultural notes regarding various aspects about deaf culture and its history.

What Impact Will the Curriculum Have?

We believe the curriculum will substantially improve the quality of ASL instruction. Students will develop conversational skills that easily transfer what they learn in class to real-life situations. The cultural behaviors and sensitivity that students learn will enable them to interact comfortably with deaf community members.

More important, the curriculum provides students with the tools to continue to learn the language in the community. This curriculum, along with ongoing ASL linguistic research, deaf cultural studies, and the production of original artistic works by the deaf community, will continue to demonstrate that ASL is the subtle, elegant, powerful language of a rich, complex culture.

Reference

Smith, Cheri, Ella Mae Lentz, and Ken Mikos. *Signing Naturally, An American Sign Language Curriculum.* Berkeley, Calif.: DawnSign Press, 1988.

Teaching French Sign Language

With few exceptions, it is deaf people who teach sign language in France. The deaf teachers teach what is truly sign language, not simply sign vocabulary or signed French, because they have their own culture. No official academic program or university training serves the teachers of French Sign Language (LSF). They train themselves through workshops held by associations like the International Visual Theater (IVT) or the Academy of French Sign Language (ALSF) and through personal inquiries and the mutual exchange of ideas. LSF teachers receive no certification or degrees. Since LSF is not taught in schools and universities, hearing people who want to learn it must take courses offered by nonprofit organizations. Aspiring teachers of the deaf have received a totally inadequate amount of sign language instruction in their training.

The impetus for teaching sign language both to the deaf and to the hearing came in 1977, at the IVT in Vincennes, on the east side of Paris. Earlier attempts had failed to catch on. In 1976, for example, some hearing people who wanted to learn signs joined a class established by Father Jouannic in Paris. He taught by signing and speaking at the same time. Others followed his example, and deaf people began taking the risk of teaching signs, often as unpaid volunteers. But many of the classes used only sign vocabulary lists, which was difficult for the hearing students. Deaf teachers had not yet developed effective teaching methods.

The breakthrough at Vincennes came from the efforts of Bill

Josette Bouchauveau is educational director of the French Sign Language Academy (Académie de la Langue des Signes Française).

Moody, who demonstrated how the deaf could teach sign language quickly to both deaf and hearing persons. Organizations soon sprang up to teach LSF, and many of them became centers of militant activity, including the Ferdinand Berthier Association in Bordeaux, the Academy of French Sign Language (ALSF) in Paris, Two Languages for One Education (2 LPE), with chapters all over France, and the Remusade Saturdays, to name a few. Soon many of the deaf who had been teaching LSF on weekends or evenings found they could leave their regular employment in offices and factories to become part-time or full-time sign instructors in the new organizations or in schools. In 1980, the newsletter *Coup d'Oeil* identified five places to learn sign language in metropolitan Paris and about twenty in the provinces.

The first deaf adult ever hired in France to teach deaf children entered the classroom of the Guiblets School in Creteil, in southeast Paris, in the fall of 1978. During the following year, the Bossuet School in Paris started a bilingual class, which served as a model for several years. By 1983, an estimated forty deaf adults skilled in sign language (but not certified) worked in the public school system.

The methods for teaching LSF to hearing people developed out of a nucleus of deaf teachers trained by Bill Moody in Vincennes, out of the Academy of French Sign Language (ALSF), and in the summer workshops sponsored by Two Languages for One Education (2 LPE). Some teachers got additional training from Gil Eastman at Gallaudet University or in Poitiers. For more than a decade, IVT has offered training sessions for deaf persons who teach LSF. Like sessions at the Academy of French Sign Language, the training does not lead to a certificate or diploma.

The growing acceptance of sign language has created an ironic situation. Schools now require that teachers of sign language have credentials, but those deaf persons who have degrees are not native signers. Deaf children therefore do not have contact with true sign language but with signs from hearing teachers or from deaf professionals for whom LSF is not the first language. This is a more serious development now, when deaf children are in the public schools, than before, when they were in residential schools where they had constant contact with older deaf children.

Methods

In meeting a deaf person for the first time, hearing persons are often apprehensive. They are confronting an unknown entity who seems incomprehensible. The deaf teacher must try to allay that apprehension by meeting alone with the students for the first time in order to establish contact. The teacher should sign clearly and simply. After the initial contact, the hearing students should be able to work with this new relationship, although the process can be difficult for some. The teacher can often reduce discomfort through exercises such as exercises in body language.

A major goal in class is to change the attitudes of the students. Most hearing people are unaccustomed to body contact, which is so important a part of deaf culture; they may even find it offensive. The teacher tries to alter this deeply entrenched attitude by establishing a formalized physical contact, for example, by having the students stand in a circle and "call" each other by tapping shoulders. Then they say "hello" and use facial expressions. Exercises of this kind reduce inhibitions about the body and enable hearing people to internalize the customs of the deaf community, which is essential for mastering LSF.

During the early years of teaching LSF, there was a tendency to teach vocabulary more than syntax, which meant that the students only learned signed French. Now that we understand the deficiencies in this approach, we have developed teaching methods that begin with an emphasis on the syntax of LSF. We do this through the use of pictures, games, stories, and role-playing. The goal is to induce hearing persons to think and reflect visually and not to translate from spoken French.

Hearing persons tend to have certain predictable responses to the teaching situation. Some do not understand why certain signs are so similar to one another, even though their spoken language has the same problem. In LSF, as in French, the same word can have different meanings. In LSF, context and facial expression give the sign its full meaning, just as, in French, context and intonation permit the listener to distinguish between homonyms. Hearing students must be led to understand that LSF is a language with a rich vocabulary and its own internal logic.

Video aides are essential in teaching LSF effectively. They may include tapes of deaf persons telling stories, followed by questions from the students about the meaning of this or that sign or about the sentence structure. They may also include tapes of the students themselves, viewed and commented on by the class. In this case, the teacher can discuss the details of sign production and enable students to step back and evaluate their work as a way of improving syntactical and bodily communication. The teacher also has a good opportunity to head off the tendency of hearing persons to inadvertently distort or even invent syntax or vocabulary.

Conclusion

More than ten years of research and discussion have demonstrated that LSF has enhanced the image and self-image of deaf persons. It has helped the parents of deaf children accept deafness by giving them a way of communicating with their child and helping the child with schoolwork and with the daily activities of being a student. It has helped individual deaf persons by strengthening their deaf identity. It has also helped deafened adults accept their condition by discovering in the deaf world a world as rich as the one they lost.

It remains true, nevertheless, that some professionals in the deaf world remain opposed to sign language. Older hearing teachers who work in deaf schools are often convinced of the virtues of oralism and refuse to learn LSF. Speech therapists, on the other hand, seem to show a slight weakening in their opposition to sign language. Perhaps the most ominous problem is the future of deaf teachers who lack professional or academic credentials. What is their role in the teaching of French Sign Language?

Experimental Bilingual Classes in France

MARTINE BRUSQUE

In 1984 and 1985, parents dissatisfied with the education offered in specialized establishments for the deaf and in integrated classes decided to set up bilingual classes in several French cities. They hoped that normal education, with deaf teachers, would enable their children to express themselves naturally and to acquire knowledge just like other children. French Sign Language (LSF), the parents believed, would permit easy communication and fruitful dialogue, leading to natural progress. The parents had themselves begun to learn LSF and had taken advantage of the early home education service that associations of the deaf provide to families. They had persuaded the local school systems for the hearing to accept a class of deaf children, meeting in their own classroom and operating independently, who would participate fully in all aspects of school life, including breaks, the cafeteria, and so forth. In this way, deaf and hearing children were placed in the same environment. These classes are still being conducted in three cities: Châlon-sur-Saône, Poitiers, and Toulouse.

The parents' association chose deaf teachers for the classes, despite the fact that the national education authorities did not recognize deaf teachers as qualified for such a position. A subsequent agreement with the authorities now permits the deaf teacher to lead the class, prepare the curriculum, teach the students, and give grades to the students. Several levels of students attend each class, the distribution

Martine Brusque is the educational director of the bilingual section, Association Iris, Toulouse.

among the levels depending on age upon arrival. It is preferred that the children arrive at preschool age and continue through to the end of primary school.

The teacher and students use LSF all day long. French Sign Language is the natural language of the deaf child and provides the freest medium for constructing and communicating ideas and thoughts. It also provides a direct means of verifying that the student really understands what is being taught and has mastered the topic. The child, through LSF, observes, compares, and makes assumptions and expresses them.

Teaching goals are comparable for deaf and learning students: the same progress is expected in language skills, in rate of learning, and in mathematics. Deaf students learn LSF first, then French, but they are constantly dealing also with written French. They do not study oral French in class but rather with a speech therapist or, if the parents desire, outside of class.

The class curriculum is based on the deaf child's identity and needs and the problems that result from lack of the ability to hear. Yet, a major goal is to make the experience of the deaf child as close as possible to that of a hearing child. The deaf student has much the same experience as the hearing student: attending school like everyone else and having his or her own class and teacher rather than a group of reeducation specialists and medical and paramedical professionals.

The parents find their role reduced to that of "normal" parents. They freely choose to place their children in the classes, the sole condition being that they must learn LSF and meet regularly with representatives of the deaf. The parents have the same financial responsibilities as other parents and in addition pay their government-provided Specialized Education Allowance to the project.

Teaching such classes makes special demands. Since education is bilingual, all school subjects are taught in addition to LSF. Video is the basic teaching medium. Children using LSF are filmed and can then see themselves, which promotes their study of sign language and their mastery of it. The students keep the videocassettes as though they were exercise books. Skill in LSF is indispensable in acquiring all kinds of general knowledge, including mathematics. For example, to formulate a problem, a video using LSF will present a story. The children will study the video to digest the mathematical concepts in the story and will then formulate the problem in written French. The basis of teaching mathematics is always LSF. In mental arithmetic, for example, the question, "What do 13 + 28 make?" is posed not with a plus sign but by making the appropriate LSF sign, which allows each child to use his or her own reasoning. The student expresses the result in LSF, and the teacher can then check the answer.

Written French is omnipresent on the walls of the classroom. When a text is studied, an overhead projector allows all the children to read it at the same time, which helps them converse more readily. Students do all reading straight from the French text and never translate LSF into French. Rather, students use LSF to discuss French: vocabulary, when explaining the meaning of a word; grammar, syntax, the meaning of a passage, or the various meanings of the same word, which the children may illustrate with examples; the requirements of each language, and the integration into French of words borrowed from foreign languages.

An interpreter is present in class when required. Preschool classes never have an interpreter, whose presence would pose problems of identity confusion for the children. Since social contacts are so vital for the proper development of the child's identity, children of preschool age attend the class where LSF is used but also, at times, classes of hearing children. Their interaction with hearing children allows the deaf children to distinguish between hearing and deaf persons and to identify with the latter.

The deaf teacher can also operate in classes of hearing children by telling stories in LSF and explaining a few signs. The story can then be analyzed by the deaf children in the bilingual class. In primary class (ages six to eleven), the deaf children remain together all the time. The teachers are deaf, though hearing teachers may occasionally intervene to resolve a cognitive problem or supply needed skills. When deaf children participate in a schoolwide activity, such as a newsletter or an outing, they use the services of an interpreter.

The class will function well only if parents establish a close relationship with the teacher through regular monthly meetings. These parent-teacher exchanges, held directly in LSF without interpretation, focus on class activities during the month and all pertinent information about life in class and at home. The meetings establish the three-way parent-child-teacher relationship that forms the bedrock of the class.

These classes represent an aggressive approach to the education of the deaf. The parents acted because they saw no progress in the previous approach to educating their children: the deaf were receiving an oral-based education at school while expressing themselves in LSF out of school. The parents wanted to make a clean break and to show that another approach, using sign language and with the deaf taking a leading role, would work better. The classes are also an experiment in teaching the deaf, who are visually oriented. Teaching must be visual and must integrate sign language fully in order to convey information and encourage discussion about the world.

The Uncertified Deaf Teacher in a Bilingual Class

MARIE-THÉRÈSE ABBOU

Approximately fifty uncertified deaf persons teach French Sign Language (LSF) in bilingual classes. Bilingual education means French on the one hand and LSF on the other. It is not a mixture of both, which would lead to confusion. French laws do not yet recognize LSF, and the educational authorities still ban the deaf from teaching, but a recent law enables parents and children to choose bilingual education.

Some fifteen years ago, when both the deaf and the hearing began to realize the importance of LSF, the deaf began teaching it to the hearing. Soon the deaf wanted to become teachers of the young deaf. Currently the deaf in France are involved in teaching children from preschool level up through age twelve.

Deaf teachers realize that they are taking considerable risks when they enter a bilingual class. They have no official status, no diploma, no teacher training; they are not fully competent in writing or in speech. On the other hand, they have grown up in the deaf world and have mastered LSF. This solid grounding has enabled them to convince the hearing of the importance of LSF and the merits of bilingual education.

The deaf are aware of the psychological stresses of working with the hearing. They work in an environment where the professionals

Marie-Thérèse Abbou is professor of French Sign Language at the Center of Language Education for Hearing-Impaired Children (Centre d'Education du Langage pour Enfants Malentendants).

(speech therapists, teachers, psychologists) frequently consider and treat them as if they were themselves deaf students and not adult, professional colleagues. The deaf must often create new visual methods of teaching, since they cannot merely transpose the methods of hearing teachers for the use of deaf students. The deaf teachers must try to participate in teacher meetings without the aid of an interpreter; they must deal with hearing parents still doubtful about LSF; they must endure criticism by the hearing regarding their methods; and, most difficult to bear, they must suffer criticism about the deaf way of life and deaf culture.

All deaf people who love working with deaf children want to improve. They improve every day, whenever they discuss their work with hearing teachers. They improve when they join discussions on bilingualism at teacher meetings where the hearing participants who have some knowledge of LSF take turns at translating. They improve further when they attend information meetings with interpretation and when they attend teacher-training courses. Outside the school, deaf teachers follow the work of deaf organizations involved in linguistic research and in providing LSF courses about teaching methods and other topics. Through these efforts at improvement, the deaf raise themselves to the same level as hearing teachers. With renewed self-confidence, they assume the responsibility of teaching, and they teach their classes with no assistance.

When the deaf become independent and responsible for their classes, they sometimes intimidate the hearing. More or less consciously, the hearing often prevent the deaf from having direct contact with the school's director, teachers, and parents, and they interpose themselves as representatives of the deaf. The hearing forget to inform the deaf about meetings, discussion groups, and of what is going on in general.

The hearing may fail to acknowledge the time required by the deaf. The hearing are usually the ones who propose topics for discussion, without giving the deaf time to prepare themselves. The hearing may post their teaching materials on the walls and leave no room for the deaf to place their own materials.

In the bilingual classroom, both deaf and hearing teachers are always present. The deaf teacher represents LSF, and the hearing teacher represents oral French. The two teachers should not work side by side, for the children would find it difficult to concentrate on one person and one language and to choose which language to use.

Deaf teachers teach all subjects (geography, history, science, mathematics) in LSF. They also use LSF to convey all essential information regarding the social and sociolinguistic environment, deaf culture, and hearing culture. Naturally, they also use LSF to discuss everyday matters with deaf children in the light of their experience, which includes virtually any imaginable topic. By placing both languages on an equal footing, the teachers reassure the deaf children, improve their self-confidence, and make them better prepared to learn French.

French Sign Language plays a critical role in the acquisition of French. It is not merely useful. First, it is the language in which explanations are given. Second, the structure and idiosyncrasies of French are taught by comparing them with those of LSF. Deaf teachers are fully aware of their limits in French, but they work closely with the hearing teacher to ensure full understanding of written texts, down to the slightest detail. When they teach, they are independent of the hearing teacher.

Unfortunately, deaf teachers still lack an official diploma that would acknowledge their professional status.

Postsecondary Education for the Deaf

Education and Jobs in the United States

DOUGLAS WATSON

What is the United States doing to assist its 1.7 million deaf citizens in preparing for, obtaining, and advancing in good jobs? And what role can training and legislation play in expanding and improving access and integration for deaf persons into the world of work?

People who are deaf are entitled to access to the best education and training we can provide so as to prepare them for their entry into a rapidly changing world of work. They should, as needed, receive career counseling, guidance, training, placement, and on-the-job support services. Moreover, our nation should continue to enact and vigorously enforce legislation that protects citizens against discrimination on the basis of disability in employment and all other activities of daily life. As we forge productive partnerships with business and industry to assist their efforts in accommodating the workplace, additional doors open for the hiring and promotion of qualified deaf workers.

Over the past few decades, our nation has been doing these things with notable success. The evidence of significant progress is indisputable, even as we acknowledge that our nation has not done some of these things as well as we would like. This paper reviews the factors that have been prominent in increasing and improving the access of deaf persons into the world of work in the United States. It will look

Douglas Watson is director of the Rehabilitation Research and Training Center on Deafness and Hearing Impairment at the University of Arkansas.

at selected issues related to advances made in training, legislation, and integration of deaf persons into the mainstream of society.

Training: Education and Rehabilitation Partnerships

Cooperative efforts between secondary and postsecondary deaf education programs and rehabilitation personnel have driven this nation's efforts to assist deaf youth and adults in obtaining the training needed to prepare them for the world of work. Regardless of whether it is assisting deaf youth in the transition from school to work, sponsoring deaf college or trade-school students through postsecondary training, retraining displaced workers, or related activities, this partnership between educational and rehabilitation programs dominates the field.

National data from the Federal/State Vocational Rehabilitation (VR) Program indicate that the fifty state VR agencies collectively serve over 40,000 deaf or hard of hearing persons each year. Approximately two-thirds of these individuals receive some form of VR-sponsored training. There have been substantial increases (17 and 30 percent, respectively) in the number of deaf and hard of hearing persons successfully rehabilitated in recent years. Rehabilitation outcomes with these two client groups in 1985 also show that 73 percent of deaf persons and 84 percent of hard of hearing persons completing their state VR programs that year were successfully rehabilitated and that they continue to achieve a higher rate of successful closure than most client groups with other disabilities (Watson, *Model State Plan*, 1990; Ragosta 1990). The fifty state VR agencies collectively now employ more than 600 counselors designated to serve deaf clients, a sixfold increase over the last two decades (Long 1989; Watson, *Deafness Rehabilitation*, 1990). These data underscore the significant role that rehabilitation plays in training.

Cooperative efforts between secondary education and rehabilitation, in the transition of an estimated 8,000 deaf youths each year from school to work or postsecondary training, are evident in data from a recent study by El-Khiami, Savage, and Tribble (1991; also

Table 1   Deaf Students' Plans at High School Graduation and Actual
Activity 12 Months after Graduation

Activity	Plans at Graduation	Activity 12 Months after Graduation
Employment	15.5%	15.0%
Rehab training	3.5%	7.1%
Vocational-technical	14.3%	11.6%
Community college	18.0%	21.8%
Four-year college	41.6%	38.2%
Other	7.0%	6.3%

Source: Watson, *Deafness Rehabilitation,* p. 91

available in Ragosta 1990). They reported that within one year following graduation from high school, 85 percent of their national
sample of deaf young adults were receiving services from their state
VR agency. The sample was national in scope and by design targeted
equal numbers of students from special schools and regular high
school programs. Table 1 presents a summary comparison for plans at
graduation of the 487 students and their activities one year later. Two
observations are in order: first, with rehabilitation assistance virtually
the entire sample was enrolled in postsecondary training programs,
except for the 15 percent who received assistance in obtaining employment; second, few of the students "got lost" in the transition process,
indicating that the secondary education and rehabilitation partnership identified and served the needs of this group of students. Major
gaps exist, however, since programs with fewer than ten students
are less frequently contacted by VR personnel (Allen, Rawlings, and
Schildroth 1989), and transition programs sometimes poorly serve
multiply and severely disabled deaf youth (Bullis, Johnson, Johnson,
and Kitrell 1990).

Studies of deaf college students yield similar findings. Between 60
and 75 percent of students report that they are receiving some form of
support from rehabilitation (Watson, Schroedel, and El-Khiami 1988;
Watson, *Deafness Rehabilitation,* 1990; Schroedel and Watson 1991).
In its audit of federally assisted postsecondary programs for deaf students, the U.S. General Accounting Office reported that for the school

year 1984–1985, "Vocational Rehabilitation grant assistance was the largest single category of assistance received by deaf students at the 10 schools" (U.S. GAO 1986, 34). Students at federally assisted postsecondary programs received over $5.6 million in VR support. Although the proportions vary by program, 68 percent (2,609 out of 3,837) of the students were receiving rehabilitation assistance. The Schroedel and Watson study found comparable levels of VR support to students in the forty-six programs they surveyed, indicating that, except for students in community colleges, VR was a major sponsor of deaf postsecondary students. They also compared the educational attainments of a cohort of 1984 postsecondary graduates from thirty-three of these programs. Their study found that graduates from federally funded programs were much more likely to have completed bachelor's or master's degrees, whereas graduates from other programs had earned vocational or associate's degrees.

The data highlight the central role that rehabilitation has assumed in the United States in cosponsoring and monitoring the education and training of deaf persons in postsecondary education and career-preparation programs. Rehabilitation, done in close cooperation with secondary education programs, as well as postsecondary education and training programs throughout the fifty states and territories of the nation, has become almost synonymous with career preparation and training of deaf youth and adults.

Until the early 1960s, Gallaudet University was the only postsecondary program in the nation designed specifically to meet the unique communication and educational needs of deaf persons. In the last three decades, an estimated 150 other postsecondary programs have opened their doors by establishing special programs for hearing-impaired students. More than 10,000 deaf students, exercising their newfound options of access and choice in higher education, are currently enrolled in colleges and universities throughout the United States and Canada (Castle 1990). Except in those programs that operate separate classes only for deaf students, the vast majority of these programs provide training in an integrated setting where deaf and hearing students attend mixed classes. For most programs, integration has required the use of interpreting, note-taking, and real-time graphic transcription services in order to assure communication accessibility for deaf students. For example, a national study of the forty-six largest postsecondary programs for deaf students in the United States showed that almost half of the 3,300 support staff at the programs were note-takers or interpreters involved for deaf students (Schroedel and Watson 1991). Different policies and practices shape the composition of the deaf students who choose an integrated or separate training experience, and create distinctly different educational and communication environments at each type of program. The 743 graduates in the Schroedel and Watson study, exercising their increased options for access and choice in higher education, majored in more than 160 different fields, a diversity unavailable to previous generations. Similar patterns of integrated enrollments are evident in other types of postsecondary training programs as well. Comprehensive rehabilitation-center training programs, vocational-technical and trade training programs, proprietary training programs, supported employment training programs, and related efforts throughout the nation are primarily integrated programs, where a small number of deaf students train alongside hearing peers.

Legislation

On July 26, 1990, President George Bush signed the Americans with Disabilities Act (ADA) with the words: "Every man, woman and child with a disability can now pass through once-closed doors into a bright new era of equality, independence and freedom." The ADA represents yet another landmark in legislative progress toward bringing persons with disabilities into the economic and social mainstream. It provides a clear and comprehensive national mandate to end discrimination against individuals with disabilities and extends civil rights protection for people with disabilities in private-sector employment, public accommodations, transportation, state and local government services, and telecommunications-relay services.

As the ADA begins to take effect in the next several years, it will expand the earlier Rehabilitation Act of 1973 (PL 93-112), which had established (in Title V) a civil rights provision for severely handicapped persons. The four main provisions of the 1973 Rehabilitation Act included

Section 501—affirmative action programs for employment, placement, and advancement of individuals with disabilities within the federal government

Section 502—creation of the Architectural and Transportation Barrier Compliance Board

Section 503—affirmative action programs for employment, placement, and advancement of severely handicapped individuals by contractors receiving federal contributions in excess of $2,500

Section 504—nondiscrimination for programs and activities receiving or benefiting from federal financial assistance

The fundamental gains deaf persons have achieved in civil rights, educational practices, communication accommodations, training, employment, career advancement, and social and community accessibility from various federal legislative and funding initiatives over the past two decades will be extended into all realms of the private sector (see Table 2 for a list of selected legislation and public policy initiatives).

A provision of the 1965 Rehabilitation Amendments (PL 89-333) provides the legislative basis for use of public funds to employ sign-language interpreters in vocational rehabilitation programs for deaf persons. Congress, through the Rehabilitation Amendments of 1978 (PL 95-602), authorized funding for the establishment of up to twelve regional interpreter-training programs. In addition to these federally funded programs, there are now over 100 interpreter-training programs throughout the country (Anderson and Stauffer 1990).

These legislative initiatives and related developments over the last twenty-five years have given deaf persons equal access to options and choices in all aspects of life, enabling them to become employees, taxpayers, and first-class citizens. And they have earned that right. Deaf individuals, their families, advocates, organizations, and professionals serving deaf persons have vigorously participated in collaborative efforts with others to bring about these hard-earned legislative victories. These gains have been further enhanced through voluntary efforts by both the public and private sectors that exceed the level of compliance required by law.

Integration into the Workplace

While legislation has mandated full civil rights protection, and the education-rehabilitation partnership has provided training programs, the question remains: do deaf people have equal access to employment opportunities? A careful reading of research literature on the socioeconomic attainments of the deaf population over the past two decades suggests that they do. The question is not whether equal opportunities exist, but whether individuals take advantage of them to obtain the education and training needed for the demands of the contemporary labor market. In looking to the future, Johnston and Packer (1987) report that more than half of the new jobs to be created in our economy by the year 2000 will require postsecondary training. Those deaf persons who enter the labor force with the right education and training will be integrated into the work force on an equal footing with hearing peers. Those who lack strong educational and training preparation will not be able to compete for the best jobs.

Based on the last national census of the deaf population, Schein and Delk (1974) found that deafness is not a bar to employment: deaf persons held jobs in every industry and in most occupational categories (technical, clerical, and service, for example), though not in the same proportions as workers in general. Schein and Delk also reported that, on the average, deaf workers earned much less than the national average, about 25 percent less. Unfortunately, we do not have more recent studies of the deaf population to help determine whether change has occurred in the twenty years since Schein and Delk conducted their survey.

There are, however, two recent studies that shed some light on what is happening. First, Schroedel and Watson (1991) found that over one-third of the deaf postsecondary 1984 graduates in their study obtained professional and technical or management and sales jobs upon

Table 2 Chronology of Selected Legislation and Public Policies, 1965–1990[a]

1965	PL 89-333: Vocational Rehabilitation Act Amendments • Rehabilitation center funding • Extends evaluation service for severely disabled individuals (for up to 18 months) • Authorizes use of case service funds for sign-language interpreter services
1965	Social Security Act Amendments • Social Security funds to be used to cover cost of vocational rehabilitation services for Social Security Disability Insurance (SSDI) recipients
1972	PL 92-603: Social Security Act Amendments • Supplementary Security Income (SSI) program pays support to persons who are not covered by the Social Security program and who have extremely limited assets
1973	PL 93-112: Rehabilitation Act of 1973 • Emphasizes services to severely disabled persons • "Civil rights" for disabled persons • Mandatory inclusion of clients in rehabilitation planning through the individualized written rehabilitation plan (IWRP)
1975	PL 94-142: Education for All Handicapped Children Act • Free appropriate education in the least restrictive environment for all handicapped children ages 5 to 21
1976	PL 94-482: Vocational Education Act Amendments • 10% set-aside funding for disabled students
1976	PL 94-103: Developmental Disabilities Assistance and Bill of Rights Act (DDA) • Care and training of developmentally disabled citizens in the least restrictive setting
1978	PL 95-602: Rehabilitation, Comprehensive Services and Developmental Disabilities Amendments • Independent living rehabilitation program for severely disabled persons without work potential • Title V replaced the categorical definition of developmental disability with a functional one • Authorized funding for the establishment of regional interpreter training programs
1983	PL 98-199: Education of the Handicapped Act Amendments • Funding and support for secondary education and transitional services for disabled students, ages 12 to 22
1983	President's Employment Initiative for Persons with Developmental Disabilities • Employment-related activities

Table 2 *Continued*

1984   PL 98-221: Rehabilitation Act Amendments
       • Discretionary programs for transitioning severely disabled individuals
1984   Department of Education, Office of Special Education and Rehabilitative
       Services Transition Initiative
       • Cooperative supported employment projects with the Administration of
         Developmental Disabilities
1984   PL 98-524: Carl O. Perkins Vocational Educational Education Act
       • Assessment, support services, and counseling and transition services for
         disabled students
       • Programs to be offered in least restrictive environment
       • 10% set-aside to be used for additional staff, services, etc., not provided
         to other individuals in vocational education
1984   PL 98-527: Developmental Disabilities Act Amendments
       • Establishes supported employment as a priority for state planning coun-
         cils funded under that act
       • Redefines developmental disability consistent with PL 95-602
1986   PL 99-506: Rehabilitation Act Amendments
       • Support for employment services
1986   PL 99-514: Tax Reform Act
       • Extends permanently a tax deduction of up to $35,000 for businesses
         for the removal of architectural and transportation barriers
       • Work-related exemptions for disabled employees
1987   PL 99-457: Education for the Handicapped Act
       • All states must provide services for handicapped children from birth
       • Services to include diagnostic screening, early education programs,
         special equipment, transportation, and financial and legal services for
         families
1987   PL 99-643: Employment Opportunities for Disabled Americans Act
       • Continued cash payments and/or Medicaid coverage to Supplemental
         Security Income (SSI) recipients who work
1990   PL 101-336: Americans with Disabilities Act
       • Extends civil rights protection to disabled individuals that are like those
         provided to individuals on the basis of race, sex, national origin, and
         religion
       • Guarantees equal opportunity to individuals in employment, public ac-
         commodations, transportation, state and local government services, and
         telecommunications

---

[a]Adapted in part from Danek and McCrone (1989, pp. 8–10).

graduation. The average 1985 earnings of the group was approximately $14,000. The level of personal income appeared to be basically determined by the level of degree completed: vocational, $11,535; associate's, $11,846; bachelor's, $16,007; master's, $20,472. The authors concluded that these differences in earnings underscore the value that employers place on the various levels of education and training that graduates brought to the workplace.

A second study, by Crammatte (1987), surveyed 1,735 deaf professionals throughout the nation. Several observations from his study are worth noting:

- Median salary was $21,957.
- Salaries ranged from 2.7 percent under $10,000 to 1.6 percent over $50,000.
- 23 percent worked in private industry, government, or owned their own business.
- Most (73 percent) were in occupations serving deaf people.
- 61 percent had a master's degree or higher.
- Level of degree completed was the strongest predictor of occupational attainment.
- 72 percent graduated from a college with a deaf program; 28 percent graduated from other colleges.
- Salaries in the deaf sector averaged $6,000 less than those in hearing sector.

Crammatte found that 55 percent of those employed in the deaf sector (occupations serving deaf people) and 41 percent of those employed in the hearing sector (private industry, government, or self-owned business) had used personal contacts to find jobs. Noting that the respondents extensively used personal contacts to find jobs, the author observed that "apparently, who you know" is as important to deaf professionals as it is to hearing professionals. Crammatte also found that those who depended more on sign language for communication used deaf community networks to find jobs, whereas those with good expressive speech used more formal approaches to finding hearing-sector jobs. He further concluded that although communication remains the primary problem that deaf professionals encounter in the hearing sector, for the vast numbers of deaf employees in the deaf sector, "communication difficulties at work are rare" (p. 32).

When Crammatte compared his 1982 cohort with a 1960 cohort (Crammatte 1968), he found several fundamental differences. Many more of the 1982 cohort had earned master's degrees and doctorates; for example, 92 respondents held doctorates in 1982 compared to 5 in 1960. Comparative analyses of the relationship between educational attainment and income showed consistently rising median salaries for each college degree. The differences were most pronounced for the holders of doctoral degrees, who, as a group, had median salaries almost double those of deaf persons who held no college degrees.

Similar to trends in the general labor market, Crammatte found that the proportion of deaf females in professional positions had increased from 10 percent in 1960 to 25 percent in 1982. He related this significant jump to the changing role and increased participation of females in the work force over the past twenty years.

However, comparative analyses of earnings and communication skills indicated no changes between the two cohorts. Those earning above-average salaries in both cohorts had superior speech skills. This was particularly the case for expressive communication, as the proportion of orally communicating respondents was greatest in higher-paying jobs.

Comparing the occupational attainments of the two cohorts, Crammatte noted several significant differences. The 1982 cohort reported employment in fifty-four different occupations, compared to the twenty-eight occupational areas in which the 1960 cohort was clustered. A much higher proportion of the 1982 cohort reported that their employers were highly accommodating and supportive, indicating a more concerted effort to accommodate the workplace to the communication needs of deaf professionals. Most striking, perhaps, was the noticeable upward mobility of deaf professionals in both the deaf and hearing sectors: 141 respondents held managerial positions in deaf education programs, and 93 were managers in private industry, government, or self-owned businesses (compared to 5 in 1960).

There are obviously many deaf professionals in positions of power in the deaf-sector workplace. Deaf professionals in the hearing sector have not achieved comparable levels of power but now hold a wide diversity of jobs and are not as concentrated in certain jobs or careers as previously. As a group, these deaf professionals were pleased with their work climates. They perceived no unfair rejection or discrimination. The main discontent, expressed by more than half the respondents, was that they did not "like" their salaries or their chances for promotions (many were teachers). Communication problems, when encountered, usually occurred in the hearing sector and were generally bridged by use of note-takers, interpreters, TDDs, and related accommodations. Friendly co-workers were identified as the most frequent source of assistance.

The profile that emerges from these and other data suggests that deaf persons attain socioeconomic integration into the mainstream of society in direct proportion to the abilities, skills, education, and training that they bring to the workplace. The impact of the 1973 Rehabilitation Amendments on promoting employment of deaf persons in the public sector is readily evident; comparable changes in the private sector are expected as ADA takes effect. As the private sector becomes more and more accessible, qualified deaf workers will be better integrated into the mainstream of the larger work force.

Workplace accommodations for deaf workers have focused almost exclusively on communication accessibility, and have frequently consisted of simple strategies such as using a note-taker, informal learning of sign language by co-workers and supervisors, using paging devices to alert deaf workers that they need to go to a specified place, installation of a TDD, or similar adjustments. More sophisticated (and costly) accommodations have included the hiring of full-time sign-language interpreters, computerized electronic-mail systems for inter-office communications, and company-sponsored classes on deafness and sign-language instruction for hearing personnel.

An increasing number of larger corporations (and some smaller firms) have ventured far beyond such standard accommodations by making major investments in staff and technology devoted to making the human and physical environment "totally accessible" to hearing-impaired and other disabled employees and customers. These voluntary efforts provide a blueprint for others. Leading consumer organizations, institutions, programs, and agencies in deafness are assisting business, industry, and government in making such accommodations.

The efforts range from assisting an individual employer on the local level up to regional or national activities with representatives of an entire industry or business. Collectively, these advocacy and educative initiatives are the foundation of a growing partnership between the field and employers. These efforts will be expanded even more, since the U.S. Office of Special Education and Rehabilitative Services (OSERS) plans to fund ten regional Business Accommodations Centers (BACs), mandated to help business and industry plan and implement accommodations for disabled workers.

Conclusion

I have reviewed the developmental milestones that represent our most productive efforts on behalf of assisting deaf persons prepare for, enter, and progress in the world of work: these developments are the best our nation has to offer, so far. By no means are we doing the best we can for all deaf workers. However, we are doing some things very well.

References

Allen, T. T., B. W. Rawlings, and A. E. Schildroth. *Deaf Students and the School-to-Work Transition*. Baltimore: Paul H. Brookes, 1989.

Anderson, G. B., and L. K. Stauffer. *Identifying Standards for the Training of Interpreters for Deaf People*. Little Rock: University of Arkansas Rehabilitation Research and Training Center on Deafness and Hearing Impairment, 1990.

Bullis, M. B., B. Johnson, P. Johnson, and G. Kitrell. *School-to-Community Transition Experiences of Hearing-Impaired Adolescents and Young Adults in the Northwest* (Final Report of NIDRR Grant No. G008635209). Monmouth, Ore.: Western Oregon State College, Teaching Research Division, 1990.

Career Development Educational Outreach Consortium. *Toward Equality: Education of the Deaf—A Coordinated Response*. Rochester, N.Y.: National Technical Institute for the Deaf, 1989.

Castle, W. E. "Current Demographics Regarding Postsecondary Education for Hearing-Impaired Persons in the United States." In *Demographic*

and Large-Scale Research with Hearing-Impaired Populations: An
International Perspective, ed. A. Weisel. Washington, D.C.: Gallaudet
Research Institute, 1990.

Crammatte, A. B. Deaf Persons in Professional Employment. Springfield,
Ill.: Charles C. Thomas, 1968.

Crammatte, A. B. Meeting the Challenge: Hearing-Impaired Professionals
in the Workplace. Washington, D.C.: Gallaudet University Press, 1987.

Danek, M. M., and W. P. McCrone. The Mandate for Transition Services:
Myth or Reality? In Deaf Students and the School-to-Work Transi-
tion, ed. T. E. Allen, B. W. Rawlings, and A. N. Schildroth, pp. 1–29.
Baltimore: Brookes, 1989.

El-Khiami, A., K. Savage, and L. Tribble. A National Study of Transition
from School to Work for Deaf Youth (Final Report of NIDRR Grant
No. G008635208). Little Rock: University of Arkansas Rehabilitation Research and Training Center on Deafness & Hearing Impairment, 1991.

Johnston, W. B., and A. H. Packer. Workforce 2000: Work and Workers for
the 21st Century. Indianapolis: Hudson Institute, 1987.

Long, N. "Serving Hearing-Impaired Clients: Challenges to the Profession."
Paper presented at the American Deafness and Rehabilitation Association, New York, May 1989.

Public Law 89-333. Vocational Rehabilitation Act Amendments. Washington, D.C.: U.S. Congress, 1965.

Public Law 93-112. Rehabilitation Act Amendments Washington, D.C.: U.S.
Congress, 1973.

Public Law 95-602. Rehabilitation Comprehensive Services and Developmental Disabilities Amendments. Washington, D.C.: U.S. Congress,
1978.

Public Law 101-336. Americans with Disabilities Act. Washington, D.C.:
U.S. Congress, 1990.

Ragosta, M., ed. Progress in Education and Rehabilitation of Deaf and Hard
of Hearing Individuals (Report of OSERS Contract No. 300-87-0056).
Princeton: Educational Testing Service, 1990.

Schein, J. D., and M. T. Delk. The Deaf Population of the United States.
Silver Spring, Md.: National Association of the Deaf, 1974.

Schroedel, J. G., and D. Watson. Enhancing Opportunities in Postsecondary
Education for Deaf Students. Little Rock: University of Arkansas Re-
habilitation Research and Training Center on Deafness & Hearing
Impairment, 1991.

U. S. Government General Accounting Office. *Deaf Education: Costs and Student Characteristics at Federally Assisted Schools.* Washington, D.C.: General Accounting Office, Report No. GAO/HRD-86-64 BR, 1986.

Watson, D. *Deafness Rehabilitation: A Major Force in Services to Deaf People.* In *Progress in Education and Rehabilitation of Deaf and Hard of Hearing Individuals* (Report of OSERS Contract No. 300-87-0056), ed. M. Ragosta. Princeton: Educational Testing Service, 1990.

Watson, D., J. G. Schroedel, and A. El-Khiami. "A National Study of Post-secondary Education of Deaf Students. In *Two decades of excellence: A foundation for the future,* ed. D. Watson, G. Long, M. Taff-Watson, and M. Harvey. Little Rock, Ark.: American Deafness and Rehabilitation Association, Monograph No. 14, 1988.

Watson, D., ed. *Model State Plan for the Rehabilitation of Individuals Who Are Deaf and Hard of Hearing.* Little Rock: University of Arkansas Rehabilitation Research and Training Center on Deafness and Hearing Impairment, 1990.

Postsecondary Education in France

JEAN BURGOS

Background

For many years, only a few deaf and hearing-impaired students, mostly those with families willing to take on a constant tutoring role, had access to higher education in France. Some of these students succeeded brilliantly. Free access to the French university is traditional. Hearing-impaired students who have passed the *baccalauréat* may enter a university, though their specific needs, especially in the area of communication, have not been addressed. Recent improvements in the educational system for the deaf call for action from those of us working at the university level. This reform will modernize teaching methods in the schools and develop "communication" as the core educative value, which will enable a growing number of deaf high school students to follow the university-oriented academic (as opposed to the vocational) curriculum.

We in the universities must initiate programs outside of our current jurisdiction in order to prepare to receive the hundreds of deaf students who will seek postsecondary training during the next ten years. We have a very limited competence in the matter, and we will have to go much further than simply modifying regulations to extend the length of studies, alter criteria for scholarships, and create special arrangements for test-taking.

The Circulars of November 16, 1981, and August 24, 1984, encourage the development of information and support services for disabled students under the current services offered to all students from the

Jean Burgos is president of the University of Savoy.

Reception, Information, and Orientation Department or from Scholastic Services. This encouragement, a sort of moral obligation, seems a timid step and does not take into account the current social and economic context. It also does not help the business world in its efforts to comply with recent legislation.

In addition to the right of students to education and of the graduates to jobs, employers must now comply with the Law of July 10, 1987, which required them to hire at least 6 percent of their new employees from among the disabled beginning in 1991. Many of the jobs for these new employees require applicants to have at least two years of postsecondary study (bac + 2). Since we currently count only six disabled students per thousand in higher education, we wonder how companies and businesses will deal with a law that mandates a quota that is ten times higher.

The Philosophy of Support Services

Measures taken in the United States and by some of our European neighbors suggest that (1) deafness leads to a communication deficiency that must be overcome through specific support services and aides to accompany the deaf student in higher education and (2) the use of training strategies oriented toward employment and a policy of sensitizing employers give hope for improved social and professional integration. Statistics published in 1987 by the National Center on Deafness of California State University show what is possible in the placement of deaf students who receive degrees. The data show that of the deaf students who graduated, 70 percent went into business and industry, with much smaller segments going into special education (10 percent), public administration (8 percent), and nonprofit organizations (6 percent). About 1 percent became entrepreneurs, and another 5 percent followed various other options.

Information from our European neighbors suggests that it is difficult to anticipate the needs of deaf students who will be registering at a university. The varying degrees of communication deficiency, the different kinds of high school backgrounds, and varying levels of self-sufficiency (which translates into needs for supplementary tutoring and communication support like cued-speech coders and LSF interpreters)—all these create demands that are hard to anticipate. Another factor is that when the number of deaf students in a given field is small (fewer than ten), the Support Services Center must take a personalized approach, whereas, later on, as the number of deaf students increases, it may be possible to group them more efficiently by field.

We are now developing support-service guidelines for a pilot program that can serve as a model for campuses around the country. The general rule is that course content must be the same for both deaf and hearing students, except for a few minor adjustments, such as provisions that deaf students have more time to take examinations and be permitted to demonstrate foreign-language competency solely in writing.

We must develop specific measures that address each disability, including deafness. They include appropriate communications media, such as video libraries with subtitles, closed-captioned decoders, telephone message services, educative computer programs, acoustic band equipment in the classroom, and so on. We need to do all this while remaining aware of the considerable variety of needs and interests of the deaf student population.

The guidelines we are developing envision providing deaf students with aides, including note-takers and tutors. Programs of this sort have begun in Lyon, Nantes, Bordeaux, Pau, Montpellier, Annecy, Chambéry, and recently in the Paris metropolitan area, thanks to cooperation and initiatives at the local level. In addition, sign-language interpreters are being provided when requested.

Accompanying Aides

The tutor for a particular department or field coordinates support services for the deaf students. The tutor, who is familiar with each student's needs, organizes the various support services, which means briefing the hearing students and faculty on the needs of deaf students, hiring and overseeing the support team, and serving as liaison with the Resource Center. The support team may include note-takers, who transcribe lectures and other classroom information, and faculty or teaching assistants who check the notes for accuracy. Deaf students receive photocopy privileges enabling them to copy notes during the day. For labs or projects outside of class, it is crucial to join the deaf student with a hearing student. The hearing student becomes an additional mediator between faculty member and student.

We have been cautious in our use of interpreters, not because we reject LSF but because the service has to be extended only to students who have mastered it (which is not the case for most students) and with interpreters who are qualified at the university level, which means, among other things, that they know the subject matter well enough to avoid translation errors. No program exists to train interpreters for this kind of work, so we have used interpreters experienced in one-on-one situations, such as aiding deaf persons in dealings with government agencies. While Title 33 of the Law of January 18, 1991, establishes the student's right to choose between an education in sign language and French or an oralist education, it is our responsibility to show that the choice can work by hiring only the most competent interpreters. The Postgraduate School of Interpreters and Translators (ESIT) in Paris will be our source for interpreters trained specifically to work in higher education.

The support services for the deaf may also include cued speech, which is not a language but an easily learned manual code designed to ease the difficulties of lipreading. Cued speech does not seem to be practiced in postsecondary institutions, but that may change in the coming years because some deaf high school students now practice it.

The University of Savoy recently signed a contract with the Ministry of National Education to develop a model program for postsecondary education for deaf students. Since the fall of 1990, a Center on Higher Learning for Hearing-Impaired Students has provided support for approximately fifteen associate-degree students in mathematics, life sciences, economics and technology, history, geography, psychology, and contemporary literature. The services extend also to a major in business techniques at the IUT (higher technical) level. The university will soon establish a multidisciplinary center to develop theoretical and applied research centered on three areas: communication, cognitive development, and the imagination. The university will begin an LSF interpreter-training program and will start a Center of Preparation for Higher Learning, which will act as a liaison with secondary schools and will later begin a year of preparatory studies for deaf students who need it. These measures will enable the University of Savoy to experiment with innovative support services and to fulfill its obligation as a model program. The ultimate goal of the Ministry of Education is to create a national network of resource centers for deaf students.

Funding for the initial efforts, involving some forty students in the academic year 1990–1991, came largely through the efforts of the nonprofit Centre Européen d'Intégration et de Préparation des Sourds à l'Enseignmement Supérieur (CESENS) and its local partners: CIFAS for Nantes, CESENS for the southwest area, ARIEDA for Montpellier, and ANPEDA for the Paris metropolitan area. The work of these organizations has sensitized local governments to the matter and persuaded them to provide equipment for improved access. The associations also secured the involvement of employers, who must comply with the new law mandating the hiring of disabled workers. Finally, the partner associations obtained financial support from the Fondation de France and major corporations like IBM France and Hewlett Packard.

The financial contributions are vital to the program's continued success. On average, each deaf student requires about 50,000 francs per academic year in additional support, as compared with an annual cost for educating hearing students of about 7,000 francs. The number of deaf students was expected to double for the 1991–1992 year, and the Ministry of National Education agreed to provide additional funding.

Conclusion

The wheels of progress are moving. We had to prove that progress was possible by overcoming the inertia of those wheels, and now the path is open, but we must keep rolling along so that our efforts, which to some people seem exceptional or idiosyncratic, become part of everyday life and thought. To the structural reform of French education for deaf children we must add the resources necessary for mainstreaming students into higher education, but in a way that respects their needs and thereby their identities.

Educating Minority Deaf People for Leadership Roles in Developing Countries

LINDSAY MOELETSI DUNN

The World Federation of the Deaf and UNESCO both recognize that the conditions of deaf people in the Third World are disastrous. Several developing nations have asked the developed nations (specifically the Scandinavian countries) for assistance with basic education and economic development. Postsecondary education can play an extremely important role in providing personnel for these developing nations. Appropriately trained people will then teach governments about the value of educating their deaf people and show them how to do it. The better-educated deaf population will then qualify for more productive employment, which will promote the advancement of the national economy. They become tax-paying citizens instead of an economic burden. We can train African-American, Hispanic, and Asian deaf people to become leaders within their communities and to provide leadership in the Third World countries from which their parents or grandparents immigrated. Educating minority deaf people means educating human resources that will eventually be more valuable than the millions of dollars that the West is giving the developing world in financial aid.

Higher education for deaf people today has progressed to the point where we can now provide candidates for any administrative position in both educational institutions and social service agencies. We can

Lindsay Moeletsi Dunn is unit director of the residence education department at the Mississippi School for the Deaf.

provide trained legal experts, linguists, social workers, and psychologists—in short, professionally trained candidates for just about any type of responsibility. W. E. B. DuBois spoke of "the talented tenth," who would be responsible for providing leadership in the black community. The talented tenth exist among the deaf also. They provide the leadership within the deaf community. Most of them graduated from schools for the deaf and went to Gallaudet University. They are now coming out of the National Technical Institute for the Deaf (NTID), California State University at Northridge (CSUN), and other postsecondary education programs. Postsecondary institutions therefore form the core around which a professional deaf community develops and flourishes.

Mainstream Higher Education Institutions

A growing number of U.S. colleges and universities are developing sophisticated support services geared toward serving disabled students, who are now recognized as an untapped resource for college recruiters. This has allowed students to choose programs tailored to meet their needs, and it has also provided a challenge to the traditional programs serving deaf students. None of these programs, however, exist within any of the more than 100 historic black colleges in the United States, despite the fact that black colleges are experiencing an unprecedented rise in enrollment. African Americans, Asians, and Hispanics are the fastest-growing population groups and are expected to increase from the present estimated 16, 6, and 11 percent, respectively, to 22, 10, and 16 percent, respectively, by the year 2000. By the year 2050, today's minorities will compose 60 percent of the U.S. population. Are we preparing for this growing nonwhite population as diligently as we prepared for the rubella children? Will black colleges be expected and encouraged to acknowledge equal responsibility? Will universities that have strong research and cultural ties with Hispanic communities be expected and encouraged to assume equal responsibility as well?

The City University of New York serves over 500 hearing-impaired students in various educational programs ranging from remedial to graduate school. Seventy percent of these students are from minorities, the largest group coming from Hispanic backgrounds (including black Hispanics, white Hispanics, and those of mixed racial backgrounds who share the common language and culture of Hispanics). Deaf students with backgrounds from the Caribbean and from Africa (continental Africa), and African Americans, constitute the next-largest group within the system. Whereas black people continue to be the majority in most major U.S. cities, they are beginning to migrate back to the South, where most historically black colleges are located. The West has seen an increased migration of Southeast Asians and Latinos. In the Southwest, programs are experiencing an influx of Latinos from Mexico, Central America, and South America. This reflects changing trends and the recognition that minorities have to be served better if they are going to become productive citizens.

Why Have We Failed to Educate the African-American Deaf?

We need to reevaluate existing programs to meet new trends. Higher education for deaf people is by no means a recent phenomenon, nor is the education of black deaf people. It has been well over 100 years since the first school for black deaf people began educating African Americans in this country. Gallaudet University began educating deaf people in 1864 but did not admit the first black deaf person, Andrew Foster, until almost 100 years later. Foster later went to West Africa, where he founded several schools for the deaf and become a great advocate for the deaf. The Andrew Foster story is a perfect example of what can happen when we educate and train minority deaf people for responsible leadership in the Third World. Reverend Foster was probably very proud of the fact that several deaf Africans earned doctorates before his untimely death in a plane crash.

Only one African-American deaf person, Dr. Glenn Anderson, and only one Hispanic, Dr. Robert Davila, have earned doctorates. We might wonder what Reverend Foster did in Africa that we have not been able to accomplish in the United States. If Reverend Foster had remained in this country after graduating from Gallaudet University and Seattle University, he would have been limited by the perverse racism of his era. By leaving to do missionary work in Africa, he had the opportunity to work meaningfully without the stigma and limitations racism might have imposed on him. He was therefore able to open schools for the deaf, train African teachers, teach ASL, and provide deaf Africans with the fundamental training that would prepare them for higher education. Among Reverend Foster's famous protégés were Dr. Peter Mba, Dr. Gabriel Adepoju, Dr. Seth Ocloo, and others who were instrumental in getting the Nigerian and Ghanaian governments to improve the education of their deaf people. Much like the Abbé de L'Epée's successor, Sicard, whose protégés (including Laurent Clerc and Jean Massieu) became instrumental in the spread of the Paris Method throughout Europe and America, Reverend Foster by his work and example trained disciples who have carried on his work in many lands.

It has been well documented that role models can play an important role in the education process. Corbett and Jensema (1981) found that only 5 percent of U.S. teachers of the deaf were from African-American backgrounds. They further noted that African Americans were simply not entering the profession. Unfortunately, the statistics have not significantly improved. Until we make efforts to change this trend, we will continue to fail in educating African-American and other minority deaf people to become productive members of the nation. We certainly cannot maintain the status quo if we recognize the important role developed nations can and must play in the advancement of developing nations.

Concerns That Good Samaritans Must Help Address

In a recent study, Yerker Andersson (1991, p. 3) noted that UNICEF had estimated that "about 80 percent of all children with disabilities in the world have no access to elementary education." He concluded that "most developing countries must, therefore, send their educators of the deaf to developed countries." Andersson challenged the National Association of the Deaf (NAD) to take the initiative "to develop a more aggressive role in aid programs for deaf children and adults in developing countries." This is obviously necessary, since the United States can afford to lend its expertise to the developing world. The Scandinavian countries have taken the initiative of sending deaf people to work in developing countries as community development trainers and advocacy coaches, to improve the advocacy and organizational skills of the deaf citizens. With the potential human resources whose ancestral backgrounds are rooted in these developing countries available here in the United States as first-, second-, or third-generation Americans, we could offer an alternative to the vast amounts of money needed to send potential deaf leaders from developing counties to the United States. African, Asian, and Latino Americans would then be instrumental in setting up "mainstreaming" programs within national universities, training interpreters, mobilizing deaf communities for political participation, and generally providing the leadership base on which developing countries could build in line with their cultural heritage. It is imperative that we be able to train deaf people in the developing world, because many myths and misunderstandings are the direct result of misinformation or just plain ignorance. One example comes from a recent study (Lane, Sururu, Naniwe 1991, p. 82), which cites an interview with a woman in Burundi, the mother of a sixteen-year-old deaf girl:

> If it's a deaf woman, no one will have anything to do with her; no one is interested in her, she can never have a husband. As soon as people see her, they label her by her handicap. She counts for nothing. . . . A deaf woman . . . her life is in her family. She goes to work for other people, for her brothers and sisters, and can never work for herself. I have no hopes for her, she'll stay at my side and when I am no longer here. . . . You know, when I think about it. . . . It really hurts.

The Conspiracy to Divide Us

Unfortunately, higher education has not yet made significant strides among minority deaf in the United States. James L. Smith has observed that

> government derives its power from the consent of the governed but not when it comes to the affairs of the deaf. We protest in vain. Our petitions addressed to governments receive no response, our resolu-

tions at national and international congresses are ignored. . . . If you ask hearing educators how they can act in utter disregard of the wishes of the deaf, they answer that we do not know our own best interest. (Lane 1984, p. 413)

People who have a significant role in the education of deaf people are not asking the black and Hispanic deaf communities how best to serve them. We have all-white national organizations that claim to represent all deaf people, all-black deaf organizations that claim to represent the black deaf community, and all-Hispanic deaf organizations claiming to represent the Hispanic community. We still have all-white deaf clubs, all-black deaf clubs, all-Hispanic deaf clubs, conferences where all participants are white, and others where all are black or Hispanic. Why have we not recognized the cultural diversity among us as an asset? Why do we insist on having our own agendas? When do we begin to recognize our collective needs and work together to accomplish mutual goals?

There are educators and service providers who choose to determine our needs without consulting us. They often use hearing people who do not represent our community but who happen to be black or Hispanic. We recognize this as tokenism, and the black deaf and hearing communities, by forging alliances within the National Black Deaf Advocates, Inc., and the Association of Black Professionals in Deafness, are committed to ending this divisive practice. This alliance is also enabling us to establish new bonds and a new understanding of deafness within the black community. The black deaf professional community, small as it is, is developing an interest in lobbying black colleges to set up support services and make programs accessible to the black deaf community. This will encourage research and will provide an environment where black deaf students can receive an education and also develop self-esteem and confidence. Do we need an alternative to Gallaudet, NTID, CSUN, and other traditional programs funded by the United States Department of Education? The United States is a democracy based on the principle of laissez-faire. Competition will therefore be beneficial and will give the Department of Education a broader basis for comparison in evaluating the effectiveness and appropriateness of programs it funds.

Black, Native American, and Hispanic deaf people continue to be placed in vocationally oriented programs instead of academic programs. In many developing countries, this remains the norm. In South Africa and the United States (and I suspect England and France, which have significant black deaf populations), very few minority deaf are encouraged to pursue challenging academic programs that can prepare them to enroll and succeed in higher education. Blacks and Hispanics continue to make up the larger proportion of illiterate deaf; they make up the larger proportion of deaf students in remedial and adult literacy programs; and they consistently score lower on psychological-assessment tests. They make up the largest number of deaf people who are unemployed and survive solely or predominantly on social security and other welfare programs. They make up the larger number of vocational-rehabilitation-dependent clients. As a result, they are often found in the revolving doors of a system that does not know what to do with them. An alternative to the traditional programs may be worth considering. Edward C. Merrill Jr. (1991, p. 95) has observed that "there is no virtue in deafness, nor in blackness, nor in whiteness, nor in maleness, nor in femaleness per se. There is much virtue in one's uniqueness and genius, if it exists, which permits that individual to draw on his abilities and to contribute to the common good." There is much virtue, therefore, in giving minority deaf the skills and opportunity to participate in this evolving global community in a constructive and productive way, much as other members of society are expected to contribute regardless of racial, religious, ethnic, sexual, or handicapping condition.

Appeals on behalf of minority deaf can be found in popular literature on deafness. The works of Donald Moores, Gilbert Delgado, Glenn Anderson, Frank Bowe, Linwood Smith and Ernest Hairston, Kenneth Nash, and others attempt to provide guidance in working with minority deaf people. A most recent attempt was made by Larry Stewart (1990), who eloquently appealed for humanitarian efforts on behalf of minorities in higher education programs. Dr. Stewart made several recommendations in his presentation at the 1990 Post Secondary Consortium hosted by the University of Tennessee in Knoxville. Below are several of the recommendations and my responses to them:

"Institutions of higher education must redefine the problem: How can traditionally underserved populations be served?" With opportunities to participate in the decision making and planning in all phases of education, it is possible to develop a blueprint for shared participation in the education of the deaf within the United States and internationally.

"There is a need to help prepare traditionally underserved populations for replacing a shrinking laborforce. Social justice demands it; it is a wise economic and human investment." Recent U.S. Census (1991) statistics place black people in the bottom rank; black males in particular have the lowest employment rate and the highest mortality rate. The black male is expected to live until age sixty-four nationally and as low as age forty-six in inner-city ghettos. This is worse than in the majority of Third World countries, in many of which males have a life expectancy as high as seventy-six years. Economic factors are the greatest contribution to the demise of the black family infrastructure. Unemployment of the black male has resulted in his inability to provide for his family, devastating his morale and encouraging him to turn to alcohol and drug abuse. This in turn has created a culture of violence. Most deaths within the black community are homicides, in which black males kill each other. Education and employment could do much to remedy this situation.

"More and better counseling and guidance for college students is needed to keep these students in school." No Hispanic or black deaf person is working full-time with this population in any program for higher education. They could serve as a positive influence on minority students at risk. Just as there is a need for more deaf counselors in all education and social service agencies, there is a desperate need for minority deaf also. The fact that the black or Hispanic deaf teacher or counselor is so rare does much to prevent a healthy development of self-esteem.

"Colleges need to expand their recruiting efforts to improve access to college for minorities and other traditionally underserved populations. Institutions of higher education need to hire more faculty members from underserved minorities." Dr. Stewart has made a very good recommendation here. Fortunately, Gallaudet University and the National Technical Institute for the Deaf have shown interest in meeting these recommendations. Both have been seeking qualified minority faculty. Unfortunately, it has been difficult to recruit deaf minority faculty because there are not enough available to compete for faculty positions. Only when institutions of higher education have attracted more minority deaf students will they be able to develop a trained cadre from which to draw future faculty and other professionals. It is imperative that colleges and universities provide appropriate support services to retain minority deaf undergraduate students and encourage them to pursue graduate studies. Incentives might include graduate internships, which would help foster an interest in a career as a university or college instructor. There would be a larger number of minority faculty and staff available, who would in turn assist in recruiting and retaining other minority students. They would also be able to serve in developing countries as technical advisers and researchers. They would then be able to play a significant role in the development of the Third World as well as their own communities.

"Make the college a part of the community through community outreach and interaction." No institution of higher education has been able to make the black and Hispanic deaf communities feel welcome and comfortable. These institutions should hold cultural and academic activities and events to encourage the target communities to participate. They should be designed to interest white deaf people also, who would learn more about other cultures and be better able to appreciate cultural diversity. Such culturally sensitive activity also helps the minority students appreciate and feel comfortable with their ethnic culture, and it enhances self-esteem.

Is There a Way Out?

It is economical and sensible to train minority deaf to become effective ambassadors, teachers, social workers, advocates, and researchers, who will then assist the developing nations. Unfortunately, the constant tuition increases at Gallaudet University and other institutions of higher education are doing more harm than good, by preventing gifted Third World and economically disadvantaged students from attaining a higher education. If tuition in U.S. universities has to be three times higher for international students, we should make efforts to work with other Western governments, international foundations, international business corporations, and religious organizations to include scholarships specifically for deaf students with the foreign aid that Third World countries receive. These scholarships should encourage them to return home by containing a clause promising jobs that correspond to the training received in the West. We need to foster environments where skills will be used effectively so that international students will want to return to their native countries. Often these people work hard to save some money, and when they eventually have enough to come to Gallaudet and other colleges, they become reluctant and afraid to return to their native countries and local communities, because their native countries do not recognize their skills because they are deaf. In some countries, deaf people still are not allowed to teach or be social workers. A determined effort to educate minority deaf in Western nations will, in the long run, provide a more realistic likelihood of assisting in the rapid development of the Third World's deaf communities.

References

Andersson, Yerker. *Perspectives on Deafness: A Deaf American Monograph.* Volume 41, nos. 1–2. Silver Spring, Md.: National Association of the Deaf, 1991.

Ashmore, Donnel H., and Wendel H. Barnes, eds. *Proceedings: 4th Biennial Regional Conference on Post Secondary Education for Hearing Impaired Persons.* Knoxville: University of Tennessee Press, 1990.

Corbett, Jr., Edward E., and Carl J. Jensema. "Teachers of the Deaf: Descriptive Profiles." Washington, D.C.: Gallaudet University Press, 1981.

Lane, Harlan. *When the Mind Hears: A History of the Deaf.* New York: Random House, 1990.

Lane, Harlan, Assumpta Naniwe, and Adolphe Sururu. *Perspectives on Deafness: A Deaf Monograph.* Volume 41, nos. 1–2. Silver Spring, Md.: National Association of the Deaf, 1991.

Merrill, Jr., Edward C. *Perspectives on Deafness: A Deaf American Monograph.* Volume 41, nos. 1–2. Silver Spring, Md.: National Association of the Deaf, 1991.

Access and Integration

Legal and Governmental Regulations Affecting Social Access for the Deaf in the United States

ROBERT R. DAVILA

Today, deaf Americans enjoy more opportunities than ever before. People who are deaf now obtain advanced degrees with greater frequency. We run businesses. We become doctors and lawyers. We are actors, and we are government officials. But this was not always true. When I started my career more than thirty-five years ago, there were few professional opportunities for deaf people. These changes have taken place in my lifetime, and I would like to discuss how deaf Americans got where we are today.

Today, in the United States, the individuals at the highest levels of government—the president, Congress, and senior government officials—are committed to a policy of promoting maximum independence for people with disabilities. And we have followed through on that commitment by enacting some of the strongest civil rights legislation in the world. These statutes, which provide access and entitlement guarantees, give deaf people and people with other disabilities the tools we need to maximize our participation in American life. Of course, statutes do not count; results do. We in the American deaf community still have much work to do to make sure that all children and adults with disabilities, including people who are deaf, reap the full benefit of our laws and regulations.

Robert R. Davila is currently headmaster of the New York School for the Deaf in White Plains, New York, and the former assistant secretary for special education and rehabilitative services, U.S. Department of Education.

President George Bush was at the forefront of the revolution to open up opportunities to people with disabilities. During his presidency, he reached out to the disability community as did no president before him. He named a number of people with disabilities to high posts in the federal government. While I was the highest-ranking deaf person, there were a number of other government officials with disabilities, including commissioners and directors of important programs. In the office I administered, for example, three of the top five positions were held by people with disabilities.

President Bush followed through on his commitment to individuals with disabilities when he signed the Americans with Disabilities Act (ADA) in 1990. The ADA is the Bill of Rights for people with disabilities. It is the most far-reaching civil rights legislation for individuals with disabilities ever enacted, and it will affect every sector of American life. Together with other antidiscrimination laws, the ADA embodies the nation's commitment to full inclusion of people with disabilities.

Soon thereafter, President Bush and his secretary of education, Lamar Alexander, made a commitment to revitalize education in United States. Called AMERICA 2000, the plan challenges everyone in the nation to aid our schools and communities. For the disability community, the promise to reform education offered a chance to showcase our programs for children and adults with disabilities. For example, our intervention program for infants and toddlers with disabilities and their families has been studied as a model program for nondisabled children who are at risk for educational underachievement. AMERICA 2000 also focused attention on the quality of the services provided and helped to improve our programs for people with disabilities.

AMERICA 2000 and the ADA build on a tradition of legislative initiatives that have opened more and more doors of opportunity for people with disabilities. But the role of the federal government in the education and employment of people who are deaf became significant only in the past thirty years. One of the founders of the first American school for deaf people was Laurent Clerc, a deaf teacher from the National Institution for Deaf-Mutes in Paris. He traveled to the United States with Thomas Hopkins Gallaudet, an American cleric who wanted to teach deaf people. They opened the first American school for deaf students, a residential institution, in Hartford, Connecticut, in 1817. During the rest of the century, as the United States became settled, residential schools for deaf people were established all over the country.

It was forty years after the first school for deaf students opened that deaf people had the opportunity to obtain college degrees. President Abraham Lincoln, just before the end of the Civil War, authorized the Columbia Institution for the Deaf, which later was to become Gallaudet College, to award college degrees to people who were deaf. For more than 100 years, Gallaudet offered the only federally funded postsecondary program in the nation available for deaf people.

Not until 1960 did federal support of education for deaf people begin to increase significantly. The enactment of the Captioned Films for the Deaf Act, a program administered by my office that provides captioning of selected movies and educational films, signaled the nation's growing awareness that deaf people were entitled to full participation in American life. In 1965, President Lyndon Johnson and the Congress established a national review board, the National Advisory Committee on the Education of the Deaf, to report on the status of education of children and young people who were deaf. In what came to be known as the Babbidge report, named for the board's chairman, the board reported that many deaf students had low academic achievement and limited opportunities for postsecondary education and employment. The Babbidge report stressed the need for comprehensive legislation that specifically addressed the needs of deaf children.

The Babbidge report led to dramatic increases in federal support for interpreter training and training for teachers and professionals in the field of deafness. More federal dollars were allocated for vocational rehabilitation for people who were deaf. During the same period, Congress and the president authorized the establishment of the National Technical Institute for the Deaf (NTID) in Rochester, New York, to give young people who were deaf a technical training option. Like Gallaudet University, NTID was and remains largely supported by federal funding. NTID was closely followed by federal support for the Kendall Demonstration Elementary School and the

Model Secondary School for the Deaf at Gallaudet. These schools support the improvement of education of deaf children and young people through the development and dissemination of new curricula, strategies, and other innovative techniques. In addition to financial support for Gallaudet and NTID, Congress also mandated other post-secondary programs for people who were deaf. Various federal agencies provided fellowships for people who were deaf as well as those with other disabilities who sought advanced degrees.

At the same time that Congress was addressing some of the concerns of the deaf community, a national movement demanding improvements in the way students with disabilities were being educated began to have an effect. In response to demands from many sectors of the disability community, Congress in 1975 passed the Education for All Handicapped Children Act, now the Individuals with Disabilities Education Act (IDEA). At its heart, IDEA guarantees a free and appropriate public education from infancy to early adulthood for each child who has a disability. It entitles each child with a disability to education and related services individually tailored to help develop the knowledge and skills necessary for maximum independence and productivity. The act gives each child the right to be educated in the least restrictive environment appropriate to his or her needs.

Since its enactment, IDEA has allowed millions of students with disabilities to come closer to achieving their potential. But a number of issues remain. For children who are deaf, IDEA opened up the possibility of schooling in the regular classroom. As deaf people have become more widely accepted in the community, the residential school option, which was the only option for many deaf students before IDEA, is no longer favored in many school districts. School districts have been placing more deaf students in the regular classroom. Under IDEA, more deaf students are being integrated at an earlier age with their hearing peers.

But not all of the programs for deaf students in local school districts offer high or even appropriate quality. Although great improvements have been made since 1965, another congressionally mandated commission on the education of the deaf reported the need for continued reform in 1988. The Commission on Education of the Deaf (COED), chaired by a deaf man, recommended improvements in a number of areas and voiced strong support for immediate action.

My office, the Office of Special Education and Rehabilitative Services (OSERS), examined the concerns related to education, rehabilitation, and research in deafness, and took steps to implement many of the commission's recommendations. A top priority was to continue to support projects that will facilitate early identification of children with hearing losses in order to be able to intervene at an earlier age. In addition, we followed up on commission recommendations calling for increased emphasis on the acquisition of English language skills for people who are deaf.

We also moved forward with other COED recommendations, including more interpreter training. We added two additional centers to provide training for interpreters, for a total of twelve across the country. Congress appropriated $1 million for grants to train educational interpreters, who are essential if deaf people are to take advantage of the opportunities now available.

I have spoken so far about education and our obligation to ensure that students who are deaf learn the skills they need to lead fulfilling, productive lives. Now I would like to turn to what could be the most significant development of our lifetime, the Americans with Disabilities Act (ADA), signed by President Bush in 1990. The deaf community was a leader in the movement to bring about this historic civil rights legislation. With its passage, the United States has declared that individuals with disabilities—including people who are deaf—are entitled to full participation in society. The act extends the same guarantees against discrimination to people with disabilities that are now accorded to women and minorities. Under the act, private businesses and public agencies must make sure that people with disabilities have the same opportunities for participation as their nondisabled peers.

The ADA calls for a revolution in the way Americans do business. The ADA is civil rights legislation, not job legislation, of course. But it requires many employers to take affirmative steps to accommodate qualified workers who are disabled. One of the most exciting developments of this law is the way businesses are rallying to support it. Recently, one of the leading magazines for business executives, *Business Week*, began an advertising campaign to encourage employers to hire people with disabilities. In the federal government, we are providing technical assistance to the business community to ensure that qualified individuals with disabilities are not shut out of the workplace.

The ADA covers more than employment. For example, every theater, restaurant, museum, lawyer's office—any business that provides services to the public—must provide equal access for everyone, including people who are deaf. No company is exempt unless it can show that compliance would result in severe economic hardship. Hotels, for example, must provide telecommunications devices for the deaf (TDDs), television sets with closed-caption decoders, and light signals to warn about emergencies. Transportation services must be made accessible to deaf persons through better visual notification and printed schedules.

For people who are deaf, the ADA will finally make the telephone fully accessible. By July 1993, all telephone companies will have established relay services so that people who are deaf and hard of hearing can use TDDs to make telephone calls to anyone in the United States, including people who do not have the special equipment. Hotels, airports, and shopping centers must have at least some telephones that can be used by people who are deaf. Under the law, none of these services can cost more than services for people without hearing impairments. Another important requirement of the ADA is that the three-digit emergency telephone number, which provides instant access to the police and the fire department, must be accessible. This will enable deaf people to report emergencies.

I have highlighted only a few of the ADA's provisions, but I have tried to convey the impact of this law on the lives of deaf Americans. From the trivial to the monumental, the ADA signals a major social change. Truly we are entering the age of empowerment for individuals with disabilities. The ADA, the IDEA, and AMERICA 2000 bring us closer to the day when individuals will not be judged by their disabilities but solely by their abilities. This is the true meaning of social integration.

I started this presentation by noting that in the United States the commitment to a policy of maximum independence reaches the highest levels. In his first month in office, President Bush called a group of individuals with disabilities, including me, to his White House office to meet with him for coffee and to identify needs and issues.

The occasion marked the first time in the history of the nation that a president made that kind of commitment to the disability community. President Bush demonstrated his commitment in many ways. Aside from the legislative initiatives that will improve the quality of life for people who are deaf for years to come, my own appointment as assistant secretary of the government agency that administers major federal programs serving more than 35 million individuals with disabilities symbolized the president's recognition of the needs and goals of all people with disabilities, including those of us who are deaf or hard of hearing. Whether we are government officials, advocates, or just interested people, now we all have the opportunity to turn statutory promises into meaningful results for individuals with disabilities. Statutes promise us access, and we must ensure that deaf people are fully included in American life.

Regulations Affecting Social Access for the Deaf in France

JEAN-PIERRE BOUILLON

The deaf in France are benefiting from a fundamental change in attitude by society and government: they are no longer regarded as patients in need of treatment but as citizens with the right to live full lives. The deaf are now receiving the attention of government agencies and ministries that address the needs of the whole nation, not just the needs of the handicapped. It remains true, nevertheless, that the two agencies most involved in providing for the deaf are the Ministry of National Education and the Ministry of Social Affairs. Longtime competitors for jurisdiction over the deaf, the two agencies have begun a period of cooperation at both the local and national levels. As these and other governmental bodies address the needs of the deaf, at a time when the deaf have received full recognition as citizens, they are having to rethink attitudes and practices at almost every turn.

Education of the deaf has received increasing attention during the past fifteen years. Of the approximately 340,000 disabled students of school age in France, 9,100 are deaf. The government has established a range of laws and regulations to provide for the education of all disabled students, including the deaf. Laws passed in 1975 and later have mandated public education for all disabled children and have provided monthly benefits and supplements. Since October 1990, the University of Chambéry, in southeastern France, has been accept-

Jean-Pierre Bouillon is honorary technical inspector for public and private schools for the hearing and sight impaired, National Human Services Agency (Direction de l'Action Sociale).

ing deaf students. The Social Security administration pays all education expenses not under the jurisdiction of the Ministry of Education and the Ministry of Social Affairs. For a semi-boarding student, the annual charge varies between 50,000 and 200,000 francs; for a full-boarding student, between 100,000 and 340,000 francs. France spends approximately one billion francs a year for the education of deaf students.

The laws of recent years have also mandated vocational placement and counseling for handicapped young people and adults and have provided compensation for an accompanying aide. A law passed in 1987 requires private and government employers to hire a minimum proportion of disabled employees (6 percent). Since 1981, deaf adults have been able to draw on the services of the Center for the Social Advancement of Deaf Adults at the National Institute for the Young Deaf in Paris. The center provides employment training, assists them in adapting to society, teaches new modes of communication, and disseminates information about employment, the family, and society. It offers correspondence courses in conjunction with the National Center of Long-Distance Teaching. Unfortunately, this very useful center remains unique in France.

Article 33 of the Law of January 18, 1991, grants the deaf freedom of choice between a bilingual education (sign language and French) or oral communication. The recognition of sign language, a major philosophical and cultural change, shows that the nation takes seriously both sign language and those who use it. Recognition provides the opportunity to pose a series of practical and technical questions, such as when and how sign language should be used with deaf children and adults, both inside and outside the school setting, to help them fill gaps in their education and join in the life of the nation.

Mainstreaming has been a part of French education since at least 1975, whether in special classes or in full- or part-time mainstreaming. The Orientation Law in Education of 1989 emphasizes mainstreaming in class and in social life for all disabled children and young people under the charge of school authorities. This trend will continue under the increasing influence of the Ministry of Education, which has broad powers over French schools and can respond to parents' demands for mainstreaming.

Growing governmental support for services catering to the deaf has raised the issue of the degree to which the deaf should participate in making decisions that affect them. In general, parents' organizations speak on behalf of children and young people. Parents are receiving increasing attention from government officials on matters affecting deaf children. In a recent interview, Claude Ervin, minister of solidarity, health, and social protection, emphasized the importance of integrating deaf children socially; he commented on the essential role of the family and urged that family representatives be included on school boards. Deaf persons have had the right to become teachers since 1976, but there are as yet too few to have a significant effect on the teaching establishment.

Deaf adults have their interests represented by the French National Federation of the Deaf (FNSF). The federation's president is also president of the Association for the Creation of Funds for Deafness (ACFOS), an organization that unites the large deaf associations.

This brief review of recent legislation points to some important and promising developments. The recognition of sign language, the emphasis on mainstreaming, and the enhanced role of parents in making decisions about their children are positive developments. The entry of the deaf into higher education, at the University of Chambéry, gives them a way of entering the nation's socioeconomic elite. The greatest needs today are in seeing that the philosophical and cultural breakthroughs of the past fifteen years are fully put into practice at the national, regional, and local levels. Now that deaf children have obtained broader options for their education, we need to see that they receive what they have been promised, and that the level of illiteracy among the deaf, still very high, is brought down to the level of the general society. We need also to improve the skills of deaf professionals. For example, in 1986 the government mandated a new certification process for teachers, but today, five years later, the teacher-training school that was to provide the new programming still does not exist. Again, in 1989 the government decentralized the administration of schools and services and transferred decision-making authority to local and regional levels. This has presented local administrative and medical personnel with difficult technical problems as they deal with a minority group that is unfamiliar to them. It would be a great help if procedures could be established for transferring responsibility for schooling and services to higher levels when a lower-level entity has too few deaf children to warrant trying to provide the full range of services. Finally, we need to improve the participation of parents in the whole process of educating children and helping them enter the mainstream of French life.

Access in California: A Case Study

MARCELLA M. MEYER

Social services for deaf persons throughout the United States have been around for as long as there have been vocational rehabilitation departments: that is, for over fifty years. Effective social services, though, have only been around for as long as deaf people have been in control of them. For some of us that has been over twenty years; for many others, only a few years; and for still others deaf control has not yet arrived.

For those of us in the deaf community, the concept of deaf control, which is rooted in the philosophy "Of, by, and for the deaf," is not new. It is based on the concept of self-determination and the fact that agencies staffed and controlled by deaf persons do a better job of direct-service provision than governmental and other community-based organizations. It rests on the notion that those who are most affected are the most committed, or "If it will personally affect me or my people, I will work harder and scream louder." Some people outside of the deaf community view the concept as novel or interesting. Unfortunately, others find it intimidating. These individuals should not be in the service delivery business.

Regardless of who's running the show, deaf or not, there is a proven formula that spells success for service delivery to deaf people. Quite simply: Philosophy + Funding + Commitment + Quality Services = Successful Service Delivery.

While surviving the service-delivery game is not necessarily difficult, growing, prospering, and continuing to make change is another

Marcella M. Meyer is executive director of the Greater Los Angeles Council on Deafness, Inc.

story entirely. Dedication, fortitude, and a commitment to the cause top the list of prerequisites for successful service provision. These elements, when combined with adequate funding and sprinkled with a measure of good business sense, produce a better standard of living for deaf people.

One of the greatest challenges facing any agency today is providing quality services in the wake of major funding cutbacks. Funding, by its very nature, is much more than the simple infusion of capital into an agency. It can determine the personality of an organization. The money's origin and attached conditions often dictate the complexion, mood, and other operating characteristics of the agency. An agency's ability to maintain its integrity and its mission while fulfilling funding requirements will ultimately make or break the agency.

While funding constraints are undeniable and must be met, the needs of the people must always be the center of focus. In California, deaf social service agencies have found a formula that balances between funding demands and quality services, while maintaining the grassroots philosophy "Of, by, and for the deaf."

How the formula of funding, services, and philosophy is intrinsically tied to success is best illustrated by the challenge faced by the eight independent, nonprofit agencies—the DSS agencies—that provide services to deaf persons in the state of California through the Department of Social Services (DSS). Each agency maintains its autonomy as a service provider but also composes a strong united force as a coalition under the California Association of the Deaf.

In 1969, two students from the National Leadership Training Program at California State University at Northridge (CSUN), as a master's degree project, did a survey of the community. They recognized the need to create unity among the various deaf groups and clubs in the Los Angeles area. The result was a council of organizations, the Greater Los Angeles Council on Deafness, Inc. (GLAD), which coordinates the various services provided in the deaf community as well as addressing problems encountered by the deaf, especially communication barriers. This council, incorporated as a tax-exempt organization under federal 501 (c)(3) status, now has more than fifty-five local member organizations.

GLAD's services, begun with a very small budget and a volunteer staff of one, have grown to $2.7 million annually and a staff of over sixty deaf and hearing persons. GLAD has six outreach programs, four contracts with the Employment Development Department (EDD) in different areas of Los Angeles, an AIDS Education/ Services Program for the Deaf, as well as a Tobacco Control Program. GLAD also has a bookstore that sells publications relating to deafness, TDD devices, decoders, alarm systems, and many other items and gifts. GLAD has cooperated in getting free TDD distribution to deaf citizens of California, in establishing a relay service, and in advancing lawsuits that seek to put deaf persons on juries, obtain closed-captioning access to public broadcasting services, and eliminate police brutality against deaf persons, among many other issues.

Five years ago, the Greater Los Angeles Council on Deafness (GLAD) and her sister DSS agencies successfully lobbied for equal access to state employment services through the Employment Development Department (EDD), which assists individuals looking for work. At that time, interpreters were routinely used by the service, and many people felt equal access had been achieved. The DSS agencies disagreed and argued that interpreters alone do not make EDD accessible. They felt that deaf people, who intimately understood the employment barriers, were needed to provide employment services. Reluctantly, and only through legislative mandate (seemingly the only way government listens), the state funded a demonstration project to be coordinated by the DSS agencies whereby deaf job developers and interpreters would be housed in several offices throughout the state. The state set more stringent placement goals and funding criteria on the deaf programs, which was unfair, but in all else the programs were identical to their hearing counterparts.

Within one year, the program *tripled* the projected placement goals, and momentum was building. Unfortunately, the state's conservative government began slashing social and mental health programs, and the deaf project was soon cut, despite its success. Deaf agencies and deaf groups voiced their concerns, and soon funds were found to continue the program.

The funds had been offered by the Department of Vocational Rehabilitation (VR) on the condition that a deaf person seeking state employment assistance must first become a client of VR. In California, VR eligibility requires a battery of physical, audiological, and often psychological tests as well as an assignment to a VR counselor who determines whether the deaf person's employment goals are realistic.

The DSS agencies met to weigh the offer. The state had made it clear that it could find no other funds. Any program that did not accept VR's funding and conditions would close. Accepting the funds would add several additional steps to the deaf job seeker's process that no hearing individual was required to do. While waiting for VR eligibility, a deaf person would lose months of earning potential. Refusing the funds would mean no specialized deaf-run employment services would be available for deaf persons.

Consensus by the DSS group was essential if the group was to have any bargaining power and the strength of the coalition was to be seriously recognized in the future. After long debates, the group agreed: no contract. The VR condition had to be removed. Any compromise would only weaken services and discourage deaf people from seeking employment.

Negotiations continued, and VR and the state, in hopes of reaching a compromise, loosened the eligibility requirements, making it easier to become a VR client. The DSS group stood firm. No additional requirements were to be placed on deaf people!

The state made arrangements to close the programs. Meanwhile, a media blitz and letter-writing campaign began in fury. Editorials made their way to the six o'clock news, and international wire services were calling for more information. The state and the VR were inundated with calls.

One day before closing the program doors, the state announced that it had found alternative funding with no strings attached. Deaf persons would continue to receive employment services in the same manner as their hearing peers. Where the state found the funds, I don't know. I can only guess they took funds earmarked for another group that was less committed and less united in its cause.

Although the DSS group labored over its decision, there really were no options. Employment opportunities determine economic advancement. Economic advancement determines place and class within a society. Any roadblock to economic advancement was simply not acceptable.

In this case, state government and the VR stated that they were sincerely acting in what they thought were the best interests of all. Really, I wonder if their motive was to keep deaf people down. Only those persons whose sole commitment was to the advancement of deaf people were able to see the disparity. They also saw that short-term gain would only turn to long-term loss.

I must point out that the DSS group's status as independent, non-profit organizations allowed them to challenge the state. Had they been part of state government, this would not have been possible. Their status as eight separate entities with equal voices gave them greater influence within the government. Eight organizations also gave eight times the people-power to amass a successful media blitz and letter-writing campaign. Had they represented only one, larger, state social service organization, their voice and people-power would have been limited.

The DSS group's actions, however did more than just save a highly successful program. They gave a message to all involved that nothing less that equality would ever be tolerated when deaf people's rights were jeopardized.

Ten years ago, the mere use of interpreters by the state employment program would have been considered an accomplishment. Today, services for deaf persons have so evolved that service providers must be equally as sophisticated. History has shown that it is the service provider who is left to (1) understand the need, (2) determine the type and quality of services required to meet the need, and (3) have the vision to see beyond it. Deaf people are best equipped to fulfill all of these characteristics. This is not to say that there is no place for hearing people in service delivery for deaf people. In fact, they must not be excluded, since an "outside" opinion is needed to keep our perspective and sometimes necessary to make rational decisions for issues that are too close to the heart.

Many people ask me, "What constitutes equal access and what types of services do deaf people need?" Equal access means just that, equal. It is not any more or any less than what hearing people receive. Equal access is achieved when deaf persons can easily say they are experiencing the same quality of life as their hearing peers. This includes the same joys, opportunities, and frustrations that await each and every one of us.

At the heart of any service delivery for deaf persons lie four basic elements: (1) communication access, (2) mental health access, (3) educational excellence, and (4) employment opportunities. Around this hub of four, all issues surrounding deafness revolve, along with the services to address them. The issues have not changed in more than fifty years, only the types of services needed to improve the quality of life for our deaf community. Here I would like to review the four basic elements of survival services as we see them at GLAD. Deaf people everywhere in the world should have them.

1. Communication access
    a. Interpreter services

    Employment: job interviews, on-the-job training, group meetings, job performance reviews

    Health: medical visits; pre-op, surgery, and post-op; health education and childbirth classes; workshops

    Government: any political meeting, forum, or speech

    Legal: criminal and civil cases, jury duty

    Education: deaf parent-teacher conferences, infancy through postsecondary training, postdoctoral work, and community education

    b. Media

    Closed-captioning for all television programming with built-in decoders

    Education, human interest, and information programs in sign language

    Open-captioned emergency warning and news flashes

    c. Telephone

    24-hour unlimited relay services anywhere in the world
    TDDs built into all pay phones

Free TDD and amplified-equipment distribution to all who need it

Highway callboxes equipped with TDDs

Mandatory TDDs for every government office

2. Mental health access

Mental health staff, both deaf and hearing, who are fluent in sign language and respectful of the unique culture of the deaf community

Mental health staff who believe in the deaf person's vast potential rather than the pathological model of deafness too often described in textbooks

Full-time, qualified on-staff interpreters knowledgeable in mental health and respectful of the deaf person's culture and community

Signaling devices on each ward and in each deaf person's primary sleeping and living areas

Sufficient TDDs throughout the facility for deaf staff and deaf inpatient use (and posted inpatient TDD policies)

Specialized ward orientation by deaf staff or qualified interpreters to prevent misunderstandings of rules

Decoders on all televisions used by deaf inpatients

Sign-language classes for staff and interested hearing inpatients

3. Educational excellence

Mandatory hearing screening of deaf infants with immediate referrals to deafness specialists who will share all deaf education options with parents

Infancy and preschool programs for all deaf children

Equal access to any public or private institution of higher learning

Teaching of all educational programs by deaf persons and hearing persons fluent in sign language

Teachers of the deaf who recognize the deaf child's potential and respect his or her position as part of a unique and vital community

Qualified educational interpreters who recognize and respect the child's role within the deaf community

4. Employment opportunities

Access to all government employment offices and employment training programs

Advocacy and assistance in job restructuring when phone use is required, or creation of an interpreter position to complement the deaf person's role

Advocacy to increase the deaf person's upward mobility within a company

Access to Mental Health Care in France

ALEXIS KARACOSTAS

I am writing on behalf of the Expert Study Group on Therapy and Deafness (GESTES), founded in 1988 by a group of pioneers made up of professionals concerned with mental health care for deaf patients.

The deaf sometimes suffer psychologically, live in pathogenic family environments, or relate to the outside world only in a deeply neurotic or psychotic mode. Their suffering may be so great that it affects their daily lives, both personal and professional. Not until the early 1970s were the questions of the mental health of the deaf formulated in clear terms and the initial solutions discovered. The institutional recognition of these problems thus has a clear historical dating. I would like now to describe the context.

France lacked virtually any specific practices regarding the mental health of the deaf when the decade of the 1970s began. The deaf received no special consideration when they entered a psychiatric ward. It was not much different in other countries. A study published in 1990 by the French National Research Center on Handicaps reviewed conditions in the United States, Britain, and Denmark and concluded that, during the previous twenty years, deaf persons had in many ways been improperly or inadequately treated when compared with the hearing population. The researchers discovered that the average time a deaf person spent in a hospital was three to four times greater than that for a hearing person. The second major finding was that the number of deaf persons committed to psychiatric wards was greater

---

Alexis Karacostas practices psychiatry in Paris.

than expected based on the proportion of deaf persons in the general population, owing to incorrect diagnosis as mental defectives and to communications problems (Bouillon 1990).

Conditions were no better at the level of theory. During the early 1970s, most specialized publications dealt with the mental suffering of the deaf solely from an educational viewpoint. Articles in the literature tended to add up all the deficiencies likely to induce deafness. This normative approach aggravated the suffering of the deaf, since it reduced deafness to a common disability. By focusing on deafness, researchers ignored the central, environmental aspect of the matter. Deafness by its nature is a disability because of the way it defines the relationship between the person and the environment. The disability lies in the mismatch between the deaf person and the dominant hearing environment. Any attempt to deal with the handicap must therefore address both the person and the environment.

Attempts to build a "psychology of the deaf" rested on a cultural basis of general ignorance about how the deaf live. Almost no one in psychiatry knew about sign language and its role in the deaf community. No one knew that these languages had been banished from teaching circles for almost a century after the Congress of Milan in 1880. Instead, the oralist position dominated, by which I mean the ideology and practices that confined individual self-realization to the medium of oral speech. That position denied the existence of a community of deafness and postulated a ruthless banning of all gestural communication.

Meanwhile, alternative perspectives were already beginning to emerge. First was the formidable antipsychiatric movement that resulted from the events of May 1968, when workers and students went to the barricades throughout France to protest a variety of perceived social and political ills. Long after their postwar colleagues, mental health professionals rediscovered the violent, antitherapeutic effects of the lunatic asylum on human behavior. They denounced the dehumanization induced by concentrating patients in closed environments. They sought alternatives to traditional hospitalization in an attempt to broaden the horizons of patients who had been transformed into chronic cases through decades of oblivion, neglect, and total lack of social interaction. Many deaf patients, once lost in the depths of the asylum, now received care adapted to their new status: individuals with an extraordinary history.

The second new perspective arose from the birth of the Deaf Movement. The enthusiasm raised by the Washington Congress of the World Federation of the Deaf in 1975 spread to France. The deaf realized that the mobilization of the parents of deaf children who had founded the National Association of Parents of Hearing-Impaired Children (ANPEDA) in 1965 and of the various deafness professionals would not suffice to promote their own objectives. They were also aware of the limits of technical progress, which had only a modest influence on their daily well-being. At a time when other minorities were striving to recover their linguistic and cultural rights in France, the deaf began founding associations and disseminating new ideas.

A number of Americans were prominent in this nascent movement. The creation of the International Visual Theater (IVT) in Vincennes occurred in 1977, under the leadership of deaf actor and director Alfredo Corrado and a hearing interpreter, Bill Moody. This company drew the attention of a speech therapist from Perray-Vaucluse Hospital, Françoise Berge, who suggested linking IVT and her department, where the deaf were occasionally hospitalized. Berge had for many years been interested in finding health care suitable for the deaf, and had assisted in the oversight of a deaf man who was hospitalized in her ward. In 1978, she visited the Mental Health Program for the Deaf at Saint Elizabeth Hospital in Washington, D.C., founded by Professor Luther Robinson in 1963. In one of the wards, specially trained staff persons, including deaf professionals, treated deaf patients through the use of sign language as a means of communication in therapy sessions. The cooperation of the professionals at Vincennes with the hospital staff soon made several health care teams aware of sign language and of the deaf experience. This new cultural approach created a climate favorable to the launching of specific health care activities. Françoise Berge led a long-term program to restore communication with deaf patients through sign language and to establish bonds that had never before existed between patients and their families and social environments. This work spread to other hospitals and health care centers.

Since 1978, when the initial breakthrough came at Perray-Vaucluse, an array of services have become available for the deaf in France. In addition to the Perray-Vaucluse Hospital, which operates in co operation with a referral center in the city, the Paris region has a day hospital with approximately twenty beds, several of which are reserved for deaf adults, and another hospital that accepts deaf children. At Saint Anne, the city's major psychiatric hospital, a specialized consulting psychiatrist who has mastered sign language receives the deaf. Some psychiatrists and psychologists in private practice also receive deaf patients; others have set up a medical/psychological assistance department in the National Institute for the Young Deaf in Paris. At Orsay Hospital, near Paris, deaf children and their families may receive consultation from a mental health team that coooperates with an association of deaf postnatal specialists.

For the past ten years, the Center for Early Medico-Social Action has been accepting deaf children from age six for truly bilingual teaching of both sign language and French. Since 1986, the Center for Assistance through Work has been fostering the vocational integration of the multihandicapped deaf. A unit opened in Saint-Lô (Brittany) in 1984 for the prevocational training of deaf children suffering from serious behavioral problems. These are only some of the organizations now in place.

Most of these groups, organizations, and teams have certain features in common. Their professionals operate according to an open approach that considers the psychiatric and psychological care of the deaf in cooperation with the deaf community. This approach helps demedicalize deafness and can prevent disease or suffering induced or maintained through mistaken treatment. Such improved knowledge of the effects of deafness on everyday life can be acquired, of course, only through contact with the deaf themselves. Another common feature is the recognition of French Sign Language (LSF) as a legitimate medium of communication that must be learned by the professionals if they are to offer services worthy of the name. In this regard, psychoanalytical research has been increasingly helpful. Analyst Françoise Dolto has frequently made public statements about the parent-deaf-child relationship and the importance of sign language as a form of communication. Her views have led to the establishment in Paris of a center for receiving both deaf and hearing children. The final common feature is the inclusion of deaf persons in mental health teams. Professionals in the United States have recognized the need for cooperation between the deaf and the hearing on mental health teams for at least the past thirty years. Even in the United States, however, the first efforts to include deaf co-workers, undertaken by Professor Kallmann in New York in 1955, met considerable resistance. In France, the institutions that have included deaf professionals in mental health teams find a great improvement in the understanding of patients' problems and in the quality of treatment.

The many favorable developments in France in recent years should not obscure the major problems and obstacles that remain. Health care teams in Paris have a privileged position relative to teams in the provinces. Deaf patients and mental health professionals outside Paris remain largely isolated. Improvements seem to come slowly from existing centers, which perhaps explains why there are so few in the provinces.

One attempt to break through this isolation is now being made by the organization that I represent, the Expert Study Group on Therapy and Deafness (GESTES), which today includes professionals who are trying to improve the conditions under which deaf patients receive mental health care. One of the aims of GESTES is to spread information to professionals all over France and to help them work together. Unfortunately, the authorities have done little to encourage these efforts. The greatest need for associations of the deaf, parents of deaf children, and mental health professionals is to sensitize the authorities to the problem. This has to be done while also improving contacts with organizations in countries that have joined the European Society for Mental Health and Deafness, established in 1988.

There is a great need to place deaf professionals in more important roles in mental health teams. In most teams, deaf professionals are involved in the teaching of sign language but do not have the credentials to be involved in care on an equal footing with their hearing colleagues. This is partly a matter of training but mainly a result of the enormous resistance that deaf candidates meet from the authorities and from hearing professionals.

There is also a need to clarify the role and function of mental health care within teaching establishments. Not so long ago, the leitmotif of psychopathological theory was that deafness and mental deficiency went hand in hand. This view is largely gone, but controversy remains.

A final difficulty concerns the use of interpreters. Some health care teams use French Sign Language interpreters, something that certainly indicates progress and a recognition of the need for better communication with the patient. However, this practice has its limits. Not only is it expensive, but it becomes an obstacle to establishing a direct relationship with the deaf patient, who must communicate through a third party. Some teams prefer deaf professionals, who can enable both patients and health care workers to learn sign language. This is the case at the National Institute for the Young Deaf and also at the Château de Vincennes. Unfortunately, most health care teams do not yet acknowledge the importance of having interpreters and the need for French Sign Language.

Far-reaching, lasting changes will come only with the support of the authorities. Is it not their mission to take the initiative by defining approaches and ethical codes that do not trail behind opinion polls or try to cope only with immediate influences and pressure groups? In the field of mental health, leadership by those in charge would be the ideal way to disentangle ourselves from the abyss of stupidity into which the Milan Congress plunged us all.

Reference

Jean-Pierre Bouillon, comp. "Deafness in Children in France." Paris: CTNERHI, 1990.

Cultural Arts Accessibility

GILBERT C. EASTMAN

Early in the nineteenth century, Laurent Clerc from Paris became the first deaf teacher in the United States and, it would seem, the first deaf person to act as a French-American liaison. His dream was to see deaf people be independent of hearing society and to ensure that they would receive proper education and develop their own culture, particularly through sign language and the arts.

I have been involved in the "deaf arts" for over thirty-five years, in the area of theater, and have come to recognize their importance in deaf culture as well as the necessity of making them accessible to the hearing culture at large. I am convinced that the arts can help bridge the communication gap between the deaf and hearing worlds. Not only will hearing audiences be able to benefit from deaf culture and understand its values and complexities, but deaf audiences will have increased access to hearing culture as well.

The deaf arts will become accessible to the hearing culture only when they are promoted by both the deaf and hearing communities. In theater, art, television, video, and so forth, the role of deaf artists is an important one that must be recognized in order for the deaf arts to continue as a vigorous artistic entity. The deaf arts need encouragement from patrons, both deaf and hearing. They also need talented deaf artists to share their craft; more deaf playwrights writing plays about deaf people; deaf directors and producers of plays or films, as well as deaf crew personnel such as camera people, lighting technicians, and special effects technicians; deaf artists expressing

---

Gilbert C. Eastman was professor of theater arts at Gallaudet University until his retirement in 1992.

deaf issues in their work, including deaf cartoonists; and deaf poets, working in American Sign Language poetry, perhaps a "*Deaf* Poets' Society."

What exists now is a growing awareness of the need for more deaf people to make themselves and their talents known in the deaf and hearing communities. The deaf theater has a number of touring companies that appeal not only to deaf but also to hearing audiences. There are theater *of* the deaf, which mainly serves hearing audiences, but where deaf audiences are welcome; theater *for* the deaf, which serves deaf audiences, but where hearing audiences are welcome; sign-language theater, which chooses classical or contemporary plays to be translated into sign language for both deaf and hearing audiences; and, perhaps more important to deaf culture, deaf theater—which includes dramatic, satirical, and humorous productions written by deaf playwrights about deaf people, their language, culture, and habits—and which serves both deaf and hearing audiences. All these types of theater are important in that they are closing the gap between the deaf and hearing worlds and creating accessibility to "deaf life."

Film also provides a growing opportunity for the deaf to make their talents known. In the beginning of motion pictures, in Hollywood, deaf actors were able to find parts in silent films. Ironically, for many decades stereotypical characters were created depicting the deaf as beggars and thieves, mentally incapacitated and yet possessing excellent speech skills. When the "talkie" was introduced, more and more deaf actors became unemployed. In recent years, however, a growing number of deaf actors have performed in film and television movies or specials, destroying some of these traditionally held misconceptions. More recently, characters have been created depicting deaf people as they really are. The late 1980s found more deaf characters depicted as professionals, such as architects and lawyers.

Television has given the deaf an opportunity to show the hearing community that these stereotypes are not only false but ludicrous. Television shows for and about the deaf define the role of deaf people in society as well as their accomplishments, special issues, politics, and needs. For example, the television magazine show "Deaf Mosaic," a breakthrough in deaf television, has earned the Emmy, television's most prestigious award for excellence, ten times since its introduction in 1985. The show has deaf producers, production specialists, and camera persons, as well as deaf hosts and guests. It is broadcast on the Discovery Channel, one of America's leading educational cable channels, thereby reaching not only deaf but hearing audiences. In addition, the national talk show "Silent Network," based in Texas, has won several Emmys. Programs such as these are an integral part of deaf society and culture, and exposure to them is essential to the hearing community, which may otherwise continue to be ignorant about who the deaf are as a community and the fact that they are not the stereotypical characters that Hollywood has created.

The rise of video and video productions has given the deaf an incredible opportunity to create and produce independent videos, for local cable access channels or local public broadcasting, that depict deaf life and culture from the viewpoint of the deaf community, thereby eradicating misconceptions about the deaf.

Deaf art is also growing. The Deaf Artists of America (DAA) Gallery in Rochester, New York, was developed to exhibit deaf art and is managed and run by deaf people. Museums such as these need the support of patrons, financial and otherwise, like any other museum. A branch of art, cartooning, is also necessary in enhancing deaf culture. Much of the culture of a nation is depicted in humorous form through the use of cartoons. From the beginning of American history, cartoons have expressed ideas and opinions, political or otherwise. Deaf culture can benefit from cartoons about its culture that express humorous incidents in deaf life, issues related to deafness, and deaf politics. It is often through humor that serious issues may be addressed and more readily understood.

A new art form is ASL Poetry, which is signed and not written. Deaf American poets such as Clayton Valli express their poetry about deaf life or situations in ASL with no vocal translation. This form, almost above all others, encompasses not only deaf life but language and expression. One way that all of these art forms can be exhibited simultaneously is through festival gatherings. The Deaf Way was an international festival held at Gallaudet University in 1989. The festival focused mainly on the expression of deaf arts in new and creative ways, including manual art, theater, poetry and signed art, and dance. It literally embodied new trends and ideas in deaf arts and drew people from all over the world.

It is important for us all to recognize our abilities in the deaf arts, and not our disabilities; we need the expression and encouragement of our artistic talents. Those deaf people who have expressed themselves through the arts have opened the doors for others to follow. Both individually and corporately, they have become the role models for the deaf community and its future.

In education, national institutions have been established to educate the deaf and open the doors for them to become more involved in the deaf and hearing communities. Schools for the deaf, for example, can provide deaf role models: teachers who have stood out as mentors and encouragers. Mainstream schools, unfortunately, lack enough deaf teachers to provide deaf role models. Institutions for higher learning are sometimes even more likely to produce role models for students as they enter into adulthood and begin to realize their dreams and goals. In the United States, Gallaudet University, the National Technical Institute for the Deaf (NTID), and the National Center on Deafness (NCOD) at California State University at Northridge (CSUN) focus on the needs of the deaf in education as well as in the arts, and have provided many role models for students.

Independent associations and institutions and their administrators also pave the way for deaf abilities to come to the surface. The National Association of the Deaf (NAD), a national organization composed mostly of deaf persons, was designed to meet the needs of the deaf community as well as preserving their rights. The Bicultural Center in Maryland, run by both deaf and hearing directors, is an example of an association that has as its objective the exhibition and promotion of deaf culture to both deaf and hearing patrons. The Miss Deaf America pageant is the pinnacle of beauty contests for deaf women in the United States, much as the Miss America or Miss Universe Pageants are for hearing women. Deaf women from most of the states compete in the areas of beauty, talent, and intelligence, and they become role models for other deaf women.

The performance arts, both stage and screen, have seen the emergence of role models in the deaf community, primarily as a result of national awards for individual achievement. For example, Phyllis Frelich won a Tony, the highest theater award on Broadway, for her performance in the stage version of *Children of a Lesser God*. Marlee Matlin won an Oscar, the highest film award, for her performance in the film version of this play, and Julianna Fjeld won an Emmy, the highest award in television, as one of the executive producers of "Love Is Never Silent." These accomplishments served to change the attitudes of the hearing community toward the deaf by showing not only that deaf people can act but that they can function in the hearing world and be a part of that community. Another deaf professional, Peter Wechsberg, a director of two films about the deaf community, was director of photography for several films in Hollywood made primarily for the hearing public. Phyllis Frelich, mentioned above, has been elected to the Screen Actors Guild in Hollywood, one of the first deaf people to receive this honor.

Deaf people who become members of the hearing community help the hearing change their attitudes, thoughts, and behavior toward deaf people and their needs. New deaf role models break stereotypes and influence attitudes in the hearing community all over the world; they show that deaf people "can do everything except hear."

The attitudes of the deaf and hearing communities toward the deaf are also influenced by education through the arts—the more they see, the more they understand. Each nation, or city, for that matter, has the capability to embrace and promote the arts for the deaf and also to make the arts accessible to the deaf community. Almost every large city in the world has museums (historical, scientific, and artistic) as well as theater and television and film companies that are providing easier access to hearing culture for deaf patrons. Washington, D.C., and Paris have the finest museums in the world—it would be a shame if these museums did not provide deaf guides (first choice) or interpreters for deaf patrons to learn the history of the world-famous works of art exhibited. Hearing patrons have access to all of these things. I, for one, am an avid patron of visual art and have appreciated the ability to share in this history. Along with, or perhaps in place of, deaf guides (first choice) or interpreters, some museums may have written versions of the guide's text. These provide information that would otherwise not be available, although professional deaf guides or interpreters would be preferable.

Hearing theaters are also providing interpreters for the deaf. For example, Arena Stage in Washington, D.C., provides sign language interpreters paid for by the theater. For the last five years, the theater has held auditions for interpreters, evaluated and chosen by deaf sign coaches. The sign coaches decide who the interpreters will be for specific plays and meet with them for consultation and translation.

Television movies and programs are now available more often captioned than not, as are major film-to-video releases. And writers are creating deaf characters in their stories who more accurately depict the deaf. The deaf community is making its culture more accessible to the hearing community. In theater, vocal interpreters, called readers, are used for hearing patrons. For example, the National Theatre of the Deaf and Gallaudet University use them on- or offstage, and sometimes as part of the productions. Touring companies, including the NTD, Gallaudet, NTID, and the Fairmount Theatre, make deaf theater more accessible to the hearing community by touring different cities. Chalb Productions, a touring company consisting of only two deaf actors, presented "The Anatomy and Physiology of Deaf Bodies," a true depiction of the value and power of deaf culture, to the deaf community in France.

In television, "Deaf Mosaic" is signed for the deaf and captioned for the deaf who don't know sign language, such as oralists and the hard of hearing, and makes use of voice-overs for the hearing.

Magazines and newspapers, such as *Deaf Life, Silent News,* and *NAD Broadcaster,* often publish articles about the deaf arts that illustrate different media in which the deaf are working and examples of their craft. Deaf Awareness Week is a way for the deaf in some states to exhibit who they are as a community through workshops, programs, and demonstrations. This is usually a statewide function and helps improve awareness of and for the deaf.

If we, as a deaf culture, continue to learn from the arts in the hearing community and to express ourselves in the deaf arts, we can more intelligently educate the hearing community and ourselves, and further enhance our deaf culture. The key to making cultural enhancement occur *in* deaf arts is education *through* deaf arts. In the past, the deaf have been stereotyped, misunderstood, and misrepresented to a large degree because of ignorance or lack of education by the hearing community. However, the opening of doors for deaf artists is making the deaf better understood as a culture. The concept of deaf arts means giving the deaf recognition as an integral part of society, both deaf and hearing. Access to the hearing culture is broadening social and cultural access for the deaf. When social access is available for both the deaf and the hearing, the hearing will never think of the deaf as being "handicapped," impaired," or "disabled."

Access to Culture in France

GUY BOUCHAUVEAU

In the nineteenth century, there were deaf artists, painters, and sculptors, and there were even deaf actors, though we have no record of their work in the theater. These were truly professional artists, whose work did not differ substantially from that of hearing artists. They were trained by hearing masters, and their works carry no hint of an art specific to the world of deafness.

Over the years, these artists disappeared. Not until the 1980s did deaf artists begin to reappear on the French scene. These artists were not sculptors or painters, but poets. The deaf community was surprised and delighted at what for them was a grand innovation, and I myself was very interested. However, despite our interest, we had mixed reactions. Sign-language poems left us a bit cold and did not evoke a genuine emotional reaction. We were disappointed, though not yet able to analyze our disappointment. Now, looking back, I understand that these poems were always developed from written texts, and for me sign-language art must be created directly in a visual language and can never be simply adapted from a written text. In parties where deaf people gather, one frequently sees stories told in a very "deaflike" way in signs, which is closer to art. Deaf people, proud of their identity and conscious of their language's extraordinary richness, must develop an art that derives specifically from sign language. Sign language adapts well to the narration of humorous

Guy Bouchauveau is vice-president of the French National Federation of the Deaf (Fédération Nationale des Sourds de France) and scientific and technical attaché to the City of Science and Industry.

stories that are almost untranslatable in written French, a fact that demonstrates the specificity of sign language.

I have one request of deaf people: let us not try to translate or imitate hearing people, but let us instead develop our own culture.

Television

An important milestone for the deaf community was the appearance of sign language in "Mes Mains Ont la Parole" (My Hands Do the Talking) in 1981, a television program starring Marie-Thérèse Abbou, herself deaf. Danielle Bouvet, the hearing producer of the program, targeted the hearing public, and the work on the program was geared toward matching signs and French in the telling of stories for children. Hearing people could see the correspondence between word and sign. This innovative and quite successful program contributed to a general awareness of sign language and inspired some people to want to learn it. Deaf people had less enthusiastic reactions. They were proud to see sign language on television, but, without really knowing why, they did not quite recognize their language, much less their culture, in the program. In fact, the language used on the program was not really French Sign Language (LSF) but signed French, so that the voice-over could match the signs.

When a program is done in sign language, we, the deaf, should oversee its development to ensure that the language is really LSF and that the result is really our own language. We should not allow our language to be tampered with for the pedagogical purposes of hearing people. Marie-Thérèse Abbou was trapped between the desire to use LSF and the requirements of a hearing producer. I feel that a sign-language program cannot be first-rate unless it is planned by deaf people. We must be careful to be very demanding about the language level of these programs, because they are shown in the schools, and it is very dangerous to propagate signed French instead of LSF. The deaf community, which is responsible for the language that represents deaf people, should oversee and control programs using LSF.

Theater

Deaf people rarely go to the theater. They can appreciate the visual spectacle of a circus or a magician but not plays, where all the dialogue is spoken. During the eighteenth and nineteenth centuries, there were plays by hearing and deaf authors (deaf people who had mastered written French) that used deaf actors. Performed in sign language or perhaps something closer to mime, the plays were probably typical deaf art. Then, little by little, this theater disappeared. It was not until the 1980s that deaf theater reappeared, with the arrival in France of Alfredo Corrado, an American. Through the creation of the International Visual Theater (IVT), Corrado presented plays in LSF about the subjects of deaf identity and oppression, as well as other themes. The new theater's avant-garde working techniques seemed strange to the deaf community, which later realized the importance of the work. These early plays were also a revelation for hearing people. (It was also under the impetus of Americans that the first sign-language classes were developed in France. Turnabout is fair play: remember the work of Laurent Clerc, the French deaf teacher who helped originate sign language in the United States.)

During the past ten years, the work at IVT has evolved along different lines. For example, IVT presented one of Molière's plays with deaf actors and in sign language. The deaf actors used a translation from the French into signs to get the play into shape. The deaf public, curious to know this famous Molière, was delighted to see theater performed in LSF. The signs stood out particularly well with the period costumes, and the play was a great success. Nevertheless, it was still a hearing text, not deaf theater reflecting the deaf world. I am still waiting for a play that shows the deaf world as seen by deaf people.

Use of Interpreters

The use of interpreters in the theater and in other settings, such as museums, has divided the deaf community. The deaf public is curious and will go to interpreted performances, which allow them to see what hearing theater is like, but not all of them consider this to be art but, rather, simply access to information. I do not find an interpreted theater performance satisfying. I cannot really feel the theatrical emotion or the sensitivity of the actor's art when it must pass through an interpreter. The interpreter provides access to the text and subject matter but comes between me and everything that is theatrical, not to mention my difficulty in choosing the right moments to look at the stage or to look at the interpreter. I worry that these experiments may develop to the detriment of truly deaf theater, which is young and fragile, and to the detriment of sign language, which may evolve into something more like signed French. It is important to encourage deaf theater with deaf actors who use LSF: that is what will help promote our language and our culture.

The earliest experiments with interpreters in museums date from the 1980s. The interpreted tours were publicized in the deaf community. I was very interested and among the first to attend. After several tours, my interest abated. The quality of the interpreting was first-rate, yet I was disappointed. Communication filtered through an intermediary was uncomfortable, and there were technical problems of visual focus: the tour guide raced through the information about each painting without realizing that we could not follow the interpreter and look at the artwork at the same time.

You will better understand what happens if you compare a tour given by a hearing guide accompanied by an interpreter with a tour given by a deaf guide. The deaf guide immediately recognizes the nature of the deaf public he or she is dealing with and knows how to adjust the language level, passing from LSF to nonverbal communication or even to international sign language. The interpreter rarely has this competence, and the hearing guide inevitably has problems targeting the needs of the deaf public.

Direct contact can be established only with a deaf guide, who uses the same language as the group. After each tour, the deaf guide reworks the content or mode of expression, in the light of the most recent tour, and reorients the presentation according to the needs and interests of the deaf public. The tours are thus conceived for the deaf public, which is essential. This way of working also encourages the development of sign language, since the guide's neologisms (new signs distilled from explanations of concepts with no common sign) begin to circulate in the deaf community. The training given to deaf tour guides also filters down to deaf teachers in the schools, who use this new information in the classroom. All of this encourages a deeper consideration of the implications of bilingual pedagogy. A final advantage is that those members of the deaf public, especially young people, who do not know how to use an interpreter will receive some exposure to the experience.

The deaf tour guide is also important as a role model for the young. Many young deaf people have a negative image of deafness: knowledge is something only hearing people can attain. For them it is very important to meet a deaf tour guide, with whom they can identify as a deaf adult in a responsible position. It is important, too, for their parents, who will be reassured about their children's prospects for professional attainment. Let us give deaf people their rightful places in museums, as has been done at the City of Science and Industry and at the Louvre. It is the prerequisite for true accessibility for the deaf community.

The Use of Technology

Technical Aids for Deaf Americans

The United States continues to see an evolution in technology that has improved access for the deaf to many social institutions. Much of the technology is of recent origin, and much of it has benefited from improvements suggested by its deaf users. There are still people around today who recall the days when the deaf mother of a newborn infant would sometimes fasten an extra diaper to the baby's diaper and then to her gown, so that the baby's movements would rouse her. And fathers would awaken to a light coming on when naked wires attached to the prongs of a clothespin, snapped to the winding stem of an old Big Ben alarm clock, closed a circuit when the clock struck a certain hour. Many of these old-time contraptions were sheer survival devices, used to get the attention of a deaf person. The signals were sound, vibration, or light—the same signals used by most alerting devices today.

Currently Used Aids

The large number of aids now available is growing constantly in type and variety. They include TDDs, closed-caption decoders, doorbell signals, sound and motion detectors, baby-cry signals, alarm clocks, smoke and fire detectors, personal pagers, electric timers, siren detectors, computer modems, answering machines, fax machines, electronic mail and bulletin boards, loud-ring signals, loud

Charles Estes is formerly executive director of the National Association of the Deaf (NAD) and now serves as manager of the Telecommunications Relay Services Program of MCI.

buzzers, strobe lights, and vibrators. Some are very simple and inexpensive; generally they are plug-in devices that can be easily removed as needs change. Others are elaborate and may be integrated into the circuitry of the home or office. The more recent devices and systems can cost a lot to buy and install.

Almost all the devices are developed and marketed in response to the needs of real people. The only government-subsidized device now common is the closed-caption decoder, which has great social, educational, and economic value for users. The decoder will eventually give way to the built-in decoding chip, since the federal Television Circuitry Decoder Act of 1990 requires that every television set marketed in the United States after July 1993 be capable of decoding closed-caption signals. Recent surveys by the U.S. Department of Education indicate that manufacturers will not require government subsidies to comply with provisions of the act. At least one manufacturer is already marketing sets that have a built-in decoder. The situation is not as good regarding teletext. Only one U.S. manufacturer markets any television sets that can receive the World System Teletext signal, a format used in at least two dozen nations.

Many of today's technical aids were developed by deaf persons. Robert Weitbrecht, a deaf scientist, developed the first acoustic coupler, upon which the American TDD system is based. A group of deaf technicians in St. Louis developed and marketed the C-Phone, a type of TDD. Most of the personnel who sell, install, and train in the operation of technical aids are deaf. Deaf sales personnel are at a distinct disadvantage, however, in attracting lucrative contracts, such as sales to a state or federal agency, which draw heavy competitive bidding from manufacturers. The intense bidding by large companies often effectively excludes deaf business owners and sales personnel.

Relay Systems

One area of great interest and activity involves the telephone and access to the national telephone network. The advent of the TDD has given deaf Americans a taste of the convenience and independence that the telephone can provide. The ability to contact family and friends simply and directly was followed by the desire to conduct personal business "normally," as done by hearing persons. The past decade has seen deaf Americans press for rapid expansion of the TDD network. At first, the method of relaying calls used volunteers. A church, club, or service organization, or sometimes an individual, would take messages and pass them from the deaf person to the intended party. The true dual-party relay was born when these volunteer entities began to use two lines simultaneously, allowing immediate give and take between the deaf person and the intended party.

More than a decade ago, the California state legislature passed a law placing a surcharge on every telephone user's bill to provide for free distribution of TDDs to deaf persons and for a statewide dual-party relay service. The relay service began operating in 1987 and was quickly emulated in Oklahoma, Arizona, Washington, New York, and other states. The federal Americans with Disabilities Act (ADA), signed into law in 1990, provides that all states must have relay services within three years of the law's effective date. More than half of the states are now in compliance and the rest seem to be making serious efforts in that direction. Most of today's relay service programs exist as a result of advocacy efforts by deaf persons. In some states it was the legislature that took the first concrete steps; in others it was the public utility regulatory agency. Almost always these bodies acted under prodding from deaf persons who demanded their share of the service benefits from public agencies or utilities.

The first four years of operation have provided many lessons in the running of relay services. One state after another has learned that usage invariably exceeds expectations, regardless of how carefully the needs were studied or the preparations were made. The tendency to underestimate usage has contributed to funding crises in several states, which were resolved only through eleventh-hour legislative sessions.

The method of funding relay services varies from state to state. Texas uses an ingenious system that recovers costs from the Universal Service Charge, a kitty into which all carriers pay and from which they may draw when the cost of servicing a call exceeds the limits the carrier may charge. Some states impose a surcharge on each subscriber, while others build the cost into the base rate of telephone services. In states using the surcharge method, carriers tend to show the charge as being for services for deaf persons, a public assistance program. Deaf users, who view the relay services as a means of equal access to the public telephone system, object strongly when the services are identified as public assistance.

No relay-related issue evokes stronger feelings than confidentiality. Service providers assure customers that no record of conversations is preserved on paper or in code, except billing-related data for long-distance calls. Operators receive training in confidentiality similar to that given interpreters. Some experiments have been made in which the call of an individual is shifted from one operator to another as the call progresses, to prevent any one operator from having full knowledge of a conversation.

One unfortunate aspect of an otherwise bright telecommunications picture is that so much of the equipment is based on the antiquated Baudot code. When telecommunications companies removed old Baudot machinery from their lines and replaced it with more modern equipment, back in the 1960s, they enjoyed a substantial tax write-off by donating the older machines to the National Association of the Deaf and other nonprofit organizations. Once the supply was exhausted, small, portable TDDs appeared on the market that were still Baudot-based. Pressure from consumers to upgrade TDDs produced halfhearted efforts to include dual codes in some of the higher-priced TDDs. Dual-mode operation has presented quite a challenge to the providers of relay services, who must accommodate Baudot, ASCII, and voice in both incoming and outgoing calls, in addition to providing "voice bridge," which allows a person who prefers to speak or listen directly to bypass the relay operator.

Prospects

Despite this problem, the telecommunications future looks bright for deaf Americans. State and federal efforts about relay services have made the carriers much more sensitive to the needs of deaf persons. Whereas a few years ago the local and interexchange carriers paid little heed to the deaf, today they compete fiercely for a piece of what has become a profitable business. Regional Bells and interexchange carriers now routinely send representatives to most major deaf functions; they also purchase advertising in deaf-related publications, sponsor exhibit booths at conferences and conventions, and in other ways compete for the attention and favor of deaf persons. The relay services have also helped "liberate" deaf workers, who are now less likely to be denied employment or promotion on the pretext that the telephone is a necessary part of the job. Relay services have enabled deaf workers, business owners, and professionals to function with a degree of independence not previously possible.

The coming of voice recognition technology will enhance the current relay services, ASCII modems and terminals, fax machines, and who knows what else. We look forward to the day when automatic language conversion makes for common transatlantic telecommunication exchanges between deaf people in France and the United States. And we look forward to the day when we can say, "France Telecom, we have arrived!"

Telecommunications in the Service of the Deaf and Hearing Impaired

JOSEFINA ZAMBRANO

For countless millions throughout the world, the telephone is the most frequently used means of communication, especially in the home. Since the advent of the telephone more than a century ago, telecommunications have progressed at an impressive pace and now offer the option of interactive remote communication to the speech impaired and hearing impaired. I shall describe these new opportunities, with special emphasis on Minitel Dialogue, which provides access to remote communication; writing within an open system, with TELETEL; and other services offered by France Telecom. I shall then review product improvements and discuss the services offered in France by the new NUMERIS network (Integrated Service Digital Network), such as communication by image. France Telecom, which has a monopoly on providing telephone services in France, is obligated to provide equal access to all the nation's users.

Telematics

Telematics refers to the interactive use of telecommunication technologies. It allows the user not only to access information but to act upon it, as, for example, in the making of reservations for rail or air travel. Thanks to the TELETEL system (French standard videotex) and the free distribution of a simple terminal, the Minitel, telematics has been developed to a high level and for a very large public.

Josefina Zambrano is research engineer for the Commercial Division of France Telecom.

The Minitel terminal consists of a display screen, a keyboard, and a built-in modem. An alternative to the Minitel terminal is a personal computer (PC) equipped with a modem and videotex emulation software. The Minitel terminal is the user's tool for gaining access to the various services available. Any subscriber to the national phone system—whether hearing or hearing impaired—can use the terminal. The hearing impaired and the deaf usually choose the terminal version called Minitel Dialogue, which enables the user to communicate in writing with all current versions of the Minitel. Various peripherals, like printers and answering machines, expand the reach of the terminal. The connection of a computer terminal to Minitel enables the deaf-blind to read information in the form of typed braille.

Unlike other communications systems, Minitel allows the deaf to communicate in writing and interactively with other telephone subscribers who have a Minitel, and it also gives them access to videotex services. The terminal is rented at a low monthly rate and comes with two warning lights that duplicate the phone ring. The 3618 Service enables written communication between two Minitels. The user dials the number 3618 on the telephone and then connects the Minitel. Once the initial screen is displayed, the user types the correspondent's number on the keyboard, and the service routes the call and informs the user about the status of the line. A computerized voice tells the correspondent to connect his or her Minitel to begin written communication with the caller.

The 5.8 million Minitel terminals, giving access to nearly a third of France's citizens, are all woven into the TELETEL network, whose user-friendly face has made it extremely successful. More than 15,000 telematic services are offered. One of the most frequently consulted services is the Electronic Telephone Directory, which is the largest real-time access data base in the world. A user seeking the name of a telephone subscriber can usually have the information within three seconds of inputting the request. Other information available includes postal ZIP codes, the cost of a telephone call, or information on obtaining official documents like identity cards. The deaf can obtain information about their special needs, such as legislation, equipment, vocational training organizations, subtitled television programs, and the like.

Among the speech impaired and hearing impaired, one of the most appreciated options is the message service, whose electronic mail-box functions as a kind of answering machine, cheap and available twenty-four hours a day. Other services of interest are Minicom, the Minitel mail service; Minitelex, a telex service; TEGETEL, for sending telegrams by Minitel; ONISEP, Information on Establishments for the Deaf; G7, a taxi call-service in the Paris region; and VOCALE, message transmission by synthetic voice.

Consumers—both deaf and hearing—may choose from a variety of useful services. For example, major mail-order firms now offer their goods on Minitel; banks provide home-banking services; railroads and airlines provide schedules, availability of seats, and ticketing; travel agencies offer the booking of tours and hotel reservations. Message-exchange services permit users to leave messages in their electronic mailboxes when they are away from home. There are games, too, as well as recreational and general information services, such as sports scores and world news. The wholesale introduction of TELETEL into France has given hearing-impaired consumers greater independence.

Services and Products

Since Minitel appeared in 1986, new needs have stimulated the creation of additional services and products. The Relay Service, located on the premises of the Paris Institute of the Young Deaf, assists deaf persons who have Minitel Dialogue to get in touch with agencies, various public and private services, and persons difficult to reach through written means. The City Hall of Nancy, in eastern France, has established a similar service.

Modern society's increasing mobility has encouraged the development of a range of products, some of which are of interest to the deaf and hearing impaired. Alphapage 15 is a text-paging machine capable of receiving messages of up to eighty characters from a Minitel at any time. An Alphapage subscriber can join the European text paging service and receive written messages in Germany, the United Kingdom, Italy, and Switzerland. Minitel 12 is an answering/recording Minitel capable of sending a written outgoing message and noting messages that arrive while the subscriber is away. It can be remotely accessed from any Minitel. The Minitel M5 is a portable unit with an acoustic coupler. The point-phone Minitel is an indoor public telephone with a standard Minitel, which allows users to communicate in writing via number 3618.

Another important development has been the increasing availability of public fax machines. The advantage of a fax terminal for the deaf is that they can take their time to prepare a message accompanied with drawings and sketches. The technical compatibility of fax machines all over the world makes them an ideal medium for long-distance communication by the deaf.

Problem Areas and Solutions

Only about 20,000 of the 70,000 potential deaf users in France subscribe to the Minitel Dialogue terminal. The main reasons why more deaf persons do not use the service include lack of information about the service; psychological blocks related to fear that other persons will be critical of the user's writing style; cost, and the fear that one's children may run up a large bill through excessive use; availability of equipment; the presence of vocal elements, such as an answering machine or answering service, at the correspondent's end of the line; and lack of mastery of the written language.

It helps greatly to begin introducing people to the service while they are in school or in training programs. Vocational training workshops that teach deaf young people to use Minitel Dialogue and telematics can keep a child from feeling isolated and improve confidence in the ability to communicate. On the hearing side, France Telecom has developed a cooperative campaign with associations of the deaf and local authorities to sensitize staff persons at hospitals, the police, fire departments, and so on, about the service.

International Coverage

The growing interconnections among European videotex networks will soon create a comprehensive system. France Telecom has created Minitelnet as the gateway to telematic communication across national borders. Foreign users equipped with a Minitel or a PC with TELE-TEL standard videotex emulation software and a modem can access French TELETEL services from abroad. They can do this through an international telephone line, via the Minitelnet gateway, via the INFONET network, or through X25, the packet-switching network. International traffic amounted to 146,200 hours in 1990, 54 percent of which involved users in Italy, which has been especially progressive in the use of videotex. The most widely used service is the Electronic Telephone Directory. A Minitel user in France can access videotex services abroad by dialing 3619 and entering the country code and the code of the service desired. The United States has two videotex services for the deaf, MEET and EXPRESS, which include applications like electronic mail, information about specialized education, medical news, subtitled television programs, and direct dialogue.

Minitel terminals have been approved for use in thirty countries, including the United States, Japan, Morocco, Singapore, and Greece, and are finding increasing use outside of France, mainly by hearing persons. At the same time, however, deaf users in these countries are beginning to procure Minitel Dialogue systems and use them for communication with each other and with hearing persons.

New Developments

The future is going to bring greater interconnections between countries and some exciting new technology offered by the Integrated Service Digital Network (NUMERIS). One of the most interesting new products will be the videophone, developed for the hearing but adaptable for image communication by the deaf. Another item is a digital phone with a video display unit, function keys, an alphanumeric keyboard, and other features, all of which will be compatible with equipment like answering machines and PCs. It will permit the display of additional assistance services to the deaf and feature the caller's number displayed on the terminal screen, the cost of the call, a signal that another caller is trying to get through, and other improvements in service.

The Late-Deafened Person

Late-Deafened Persons in the United States

LAUREL E. GLASS

The many Americans who became hard of hearing or deafened as adults, at age eighteen or over, have needs and meet challenges that are much different from those of persons whose deafness or other hearing loss began before or shortly after birth or as they were growing up. At least 15 to 20 million U.S. residents have hearing losses that began in adulthood. Their loss ranges from mildly hard of hearing to profoundly deafened, and its prevalence and severity tend to increase with age. Most persons with adult-onset hearing loss are "culturally hearing"; that is, they were raised from birth with language and a communication style that depends primarily on voice and sound. Few are fluent in, and most have no knowledge of, any manual language; even if they know or learn sign language, they rarely have acquaintances with whom to practice signing or to communicate in sign language. For these adults, hearing loss is a new experience, and so is the way it hinders communication and intimacy with family, friends, and other hearing persons.

The few research studies and the many anecdotal reports agree in suggesting that adult-onset hearing loss can be significantly disabling, whether in home or workplace or community. Partly because it is invisible, such hearing loss may prevent other people from fully using the impaired person's special skills and competencies. Again and again, the hearing-impaired person is placed in circumstances where

Laurel E. Glass is director of the Project on Adult Onset Hearing Loss at the University of California Medical School, San Francisco.

understanding is necessary for function but the impairment interferes with performance, leading to isolation, loneliness, and anxiety. Intense anger is often felt because others fail to understand that "wrong" responses are not intentional, and they also frustrate the hearing-impaired person. People with hearing loss often mention their chronic fatigue, which they attribute to stressful efforts to understand speech and to their frequent failure to understand what is said, no matter how hard they try. Over the long term, they often experience a substantial decrease in self-esteem. Hearing loss acquired in adulthood is not benign.

Access to Rehabilitation Assistance

The resources available to persons who have lost hearing in adulthood are somewhat different from those for persons who lost their hearing early in life. I will address the resources from the perspective of vocational rehabilitation professionals and from the viewpoint of adventitiously hard of hearing and deafened persons themselves.

In 1986, the California State Department of Vocational Rehabilitation and its director of hearing-impaired programs, Ed Rogers, surveyed the state's rehabilitation counselors working with hearing-impaired clients. The primary concern about working with adventitiously deafened and hard of hearing clients is conveyed in these words from one of the fifty-nine respondents: "We need to know how to work with a person who grew up hearing and became deaf or hard-of-hearing later in life because these clients are most difficult to work with, especially if a career change is needed."

Most of the respondents said they needed more information and training about persons who lose hearing as adults, especially in three areas: mental health issues, work adjustments, and the kinds of resources available. In particular, the counselors said they needed help in understanding the psychological makeup of such clients and how they adjust socially, emotionally, and vocationally to so significant a loss. The counselors also said they needed training in how to help these individuals overcome their handicaps and go on living, and they asked for help in recognizing which clients need formal psychological counseling and which might be suicidal.

Work adjustments are hard for persons with adult-onset hearing loss, and rehabilitation counselors often become involved in trying to identify and mitigate problems at the workplace. This may mean helping employers adapt the job so that the hearing-impaired person can continue to work well; for example, changes in the work assignment, the addition of technical assistive devices, and other environmental modifications may be recommended. The rehabilitation respondents saw their hardest task as working with clients whose job could not be adapted to the reality of their hearing deficiency. They saw one of their hardest tasks as helping the client analyze the job market, deal with fewer job options, and develop transferable skills.

The kinds of resources available must be brought to the client's attention. These resources include places to learn the special vocabularies and skills needed for new vocations, information about where to study lipreading and sign language, and information about technical devices and where to obtain them. Since the hearing-impaired client may experience rejection by employers or work associates, discrimination against them may require referral for legal assistance. Few of these resources are easily accessible, and rehabilitation counselors reported that they themselves were unsure about how best to make them available to their adventitiously hearing-impaired clients.

Whatever the quality of vocational rehabilitation services, and however large the number of potential clients, relatively few adventitiously hard of hearing or deafened persons make their way to rehabilitation agencies. In a recent study funded by the U.S. Department of Education's National Institute on Disability and Rehabilitation Research (NIDRR), we received slightly more than 8,000 responses to a survey of persons who had experienced a noticeable hearing loss as adults. Fewer than half of the respondents answered a question about rehabilitation services; of the 3,400 who responded, fewer than half had actually applied for assistance. However, of the 1,458 who did apply, a very high proportion (87 percent) had been helped.

Since many persons with adult-onset hearing loss do not know that rehabilitation services are available, and since many rehabilitation counselors say they are unsure about how best to help these clients, there is a gap in the assistance that is being provided. There may be some hope for improvement, because NIDRR recently funded a three-year project aimed at documenting the rehabilitation needs of persons with late-onset hearing loss. The data, including information about gaps in rehabilitation services, will be used by the Office of Special Education and Rehabilitation Services of the U.S. Department of Education in developing plans to meet the needs of this population.

Self-Help Groups

Probably the most important resources for persons who become hard of hearing or deafened in adulthood are self-help groups. These are made up primarily of persons who themselves lost hearing as adults or, at least, who lost hearing after they had established a spoken, sound-dependent, primary language. Some hearing family members and hearing professionals may also be members.

As part of our NIDRR-funded project to study successful adaptation to adult-onset hearing loss, we met recently in small focus groups with a total of 90 adventitiously hard of hearing or deafened persons. No more than 5 hearing-impaired individuals were in any one group, and real-time computer-assisted captioning was used. We also interviewed individually (for about three hours each) another 130 subjects who were selected as having "coped successfully" with their hearing losses. Repeatedly we heard from respondents that self-help groups had been their most useful resource as they adapted to hearing loss. They reported that they had received in such groups accurate information, personal support, the feeling that others understood, plus workable hints about participating in conversation even though they did not hear it clearly. They also experienced being with people who had the patience to allow them *not* to understand what was said and who worked with them until they did.

There are several such groups in the United States. Most are small and serve a local membership, but two are especially well known nationally and may provide good models. The first, established about twelve years ago, is called Self Help for Hard of Hearing People, Inc.

(SHHH). Howard E. (Rocky) Stone, Sr., is its unpaid executive director. The second, established about three years ago, is the Association of Late Deafened Adults (ALDA), based in Chicago, whose unpaid national president is Bill Graham. Both groups have a knowledgeable leadership and provide accurate information about resources, including technical assistance; they also keep advocacy issues before their members. Both organizations are effective advocates for hard of hearing and deafened adults. Of the two leaders, Rocky Stone has been in the field longer and probably has a broader political base across the spectrum of issues. He engages almost constantly in political advocacy, even at the highest levels, for example, with members of the president's cabinet in Washington. Members of SHHH sit on governors' commissions in several states and on many influential local community boards and agencies. Members of ALDA have also begun to gain prominence in advocacy at local, state, and national levels.

SHHH has grown enormously since its beginnings in Rocky Stone's basement. Members are generally older than those of ALDA, include many retirees, and are predominantly Caucasian and middle- and upper-middle income. The organization's literature rarely uses the word "deaf" and prefers "hard of hearing," even in reference to persons with hearing thresholds of 110 decibels or higher. SHHH provides members (and interested members of the public) with sophisticated and accurate information about hearing-help technologies, including "assistive listening devices" (ALDs) such as FM, infrared, and audioloop amplification systems; these are able to suppress ambient noise and greatly improve the sound quality of speech. Information is also provided about hearing aids, cochlear implants, and other developing technologies. Many SHHH members use personal hardwired or FM amplifiers to supplement their lipreading and hearing aids.

Cued speech seems to be the manual communication mode most favored by SHHH, though perhaps more in principle than in practice. American Sign Language (ASL), as a non-English language with unique syntax and grammar, seems least favored by the organization's members. Contact sign language (nearest to what was formerly called pidgin signed English) incorporates some of the hand, body, facial, and directional components of ASL but uses English word order, syntax, and grammar. Relatively few members of SHHH are fluent in any manual language, although that may be partly due to decreased availability of community-college classes in contact sign languages, especially since the Deaf Freedom movement advocates ASL and the rights of deaf culture and deaf community so strongly. SHHH has been especially helpful in publicizing the work of Gallaudet University psychologist Sam Trychin, whose courses on stress and assertiveness training are cited repeatedly as helpful to persons learning to cope with adult-onset hearing loss.

Members of ALDA are generally younger than SHHH members with a predominance of people still in the work force. Many became deafened, in contrast to hard of hearing, from surgery for a tumor of the auditory nerve; in other words, they experienced sudden deafness. ALDA has been less interested in assistive listening devices than in a system it developed for real-time captioning called ALDA-CRUDE, which is available at many ALDA meetings and uses volunteer court reporters or sign-language interpreters as typists; the text is projected onto a large screen or television monitor and is accessible to all. Sign language is encouraged by ALDA, and many members, while not yet fluent, have reasonable competence at signed communication. As part of its function as a support group, the organization publishes a newsletter full of stories both touching and humorous, and encourages pen-pal correspondence between members as well as letters to the editor. From its base in Chicago, ALDA is expanding nationwide.

The annual meetings of the two self-help organizations are models of accessibility for hard of hearing and deafened persons. They provide real-time computer-assisted note-taking, often with volunteer or paid court reporters and interpreters at the computer keyboard. Such computer-assisted note-taking often uses software that displays text in large type on a standard monitor. Liquid-crystal display panels and an overhead projector are also used to transmit real-time text onto a large screen visible from most places in the room. Both organizations provide ASL, contact sign, and oral interpreters at their annual meetings, and both lend assistive listening devices for meeting participants.

Conclusion

Persons who become hard of hearing or deafened as adults have histories, needs, and experiences dramatically different from those of persons who were born deaf or learned a sign language early in life. They experience a significant loss of communication effectiveness. "Culturally hearing" but "audiologically impaired," they suffer a disabling experience. For some, whose work or personal needs depend on the interpretation of sound into meaning, hearing loss may interfere significantly with their lives. Some describe a feeling of "cultural homelessness," of being misfits in both the hearing world and the deaf world. This reality is usually unrecognized by professionals, by culturally deaf persons, and by the hearing community.

Neither public nor private rehabilitation agencies have picked up the slack in services needed by "become" hard of hearing and "become" deaf persons. Those in need of the services often do not know they exist. Moreover, there is uncertainty within the rehabilitation system about what is needed by individuals who lose hearing in adulthood, and, in any case, the range and number of rehabilitation services available are somewhat limited. Even professionals, including some otologists and audiologists, seem unaware of the range of needs or of the varieties of assistance that could be helpful to adventitiously hearing-impaired persons.

The most useful resources are the self-help groups. Appropriate, low-cost, and effective, they have helped many adventitiously deafened and hard of hearing people adapt to hearing loss. May their efforts prosper!

Self-Help Organizations

Association of Late Deafened Adults (ALDA), 2445 W. Cuyler, Chicago, Ill. 60618

Self Help for Hard of Hearing People, Inc. (SHHH), 7910 Woodmont Avenue, Bethesda, Md. 20814

References

Glass, Laurel E. "Hearing." In *Aging and Sensory Change: A Bibliography,* ed. Marcia Abramson and Paula Lovas, pp. 17–23. Washington, D.C.: The Gerontological Society of America, 1988.

Glass, Laurel E., ed. "Hearing Impairment." *International Journal on Technology and Aging* 3 (Fall/Winter 1990).

Luey, Helen S., and Myra Per-Lee. *What Should I Do Now? Problems and Adaptations of the Deafened Adult.* Washington, D.C.: The National Academy, Gallaudet University, 1983.

Office of Technology Assessment, U.S. Congress. *Hearing Impairment and Elderly People: A Background Paper,* OTA-BP-BA-30. Washington, D.C.: Government Printing Office, 1986.

Orlans, Harold, ed. *Adjustment to Adult Hearing Loss.* San Diego, Calif.: College-Hill Press, 1985. Out of print; copies available from Singular Press, 4284 41st St., San Diego, Calif. 92105.

Special Problems of Late-Deafened Persons

JEAN DAUBY

Persons who become deaf or hearing-impaired after having acquired
spoken language make up a large majority of the hearing-impaired
population. In France, the adventitiously deaf number about three
million, including hard of hearing, profoundly deaf, and totally deaf
individuals. Despite their large numbers, they find that their special
problems are little recognized by the general public and even by health
professionals and social workers. Before discussing the adventitiously
deaf, it is necessary to clarify a widespread confusion that tends to
identify the late-deafened with those who are simply hard of hearing. In fact, most of the late-deafened are afflicted with a deafness
that is great or even total. We should add, finally, that almost half of
late-deafened adults are senior citizens.

Psychological Aspects

Most late-deafened adults are persons of normal intellectual and
physical capabilities, with the usual set of social, emotional, and professional relationships, who gradually or even suddenly find themselves cut off from their accustomed lives. Friends come around less

---

Jean Dauby is president of the Coordination Bureau of Associations of the Late-Deafened
and Hearing Impaired (Bureau de Coordination des Associations de Devenus Sourds et
Mal Entendants/BUCODES).

often and finally not at all; colleagues appear less frequently; even the family environment changes. Everything sinks into silence.

The late-deafened person usually tries to deny that there is any problem, in part because our society points its finger at any deviation from the norm. The affected person behaves as if he still hears, and wishes that some technological advance could return him to that fondly remembered time of hearing. People in such a mental state have as many problems integrating into the world of the prelingually deaf, whose worldview is very different, as into the world of the hearing, which rejects them. To date, however, most psychological studies have concentrated on the prelingually deaf and ignored the late-deafened.

The late-deafened person can choose from several options in coping with the stresses generated by increasing isolation from the hearing world. Hearing aids are the option prescribed most often, but they are not a panacea, for they are not always practical (only 500,000 of the 3 million hearing impaired in France use them) or have only a small beneficial effect (for those who have little residual hearing). Except for the partially deaf, hearing aids alone cannot reestablish communication.

The second option, lipreading, is a powerful tool that allows normal or near-normal communication with hearing people. It has clear advantages over other communication methods, such as writing (which is slow) or sign language (which most hearing people do not know). Many deaf or partially deaf people master lipreading so well that their partners in conversation do not even know they have a hearing deficit.

Against these obvious advantages must be balanced some disadvantages to lipreading. It works only if the hearing persons speak face to face, not too rapidly, and with clear articulation. Skill at lipreading comes only with instruction and much practice. In France, courses in lipreading, whose cost is reimbursed by Social Security, are taught by specially trained speech therapists working at institutions, in private practice, or in classes organized by associations of deafened or hearing-impaired persons. Unfortunately, lipreading is not important in the training of therapists, and the few who master it usually gravitate to the speech training of deaf children. The consistent refusal by government agencies to support the ongoing training provided by speech therapists for the late-deafened has compelled the member organizations of the Coordination Bureau of Associations of the Late-Deafened and Hearing Impaired (BUCODES) to pay the costs.

A third option for the late-deafened person is to take advantage of the services offered by the various associations of deafened and hearing-impaired persons. The associations can help alleviate isolation by providing publications, get-togethers, classes in lipreading, and the like. Finally, the late-deafened person can use the many technical aids that have appeared in recent years, such as telephone amplifiers, electronic communications devices like the Minitel, subtitled television programs, and visual warning systems.

Employment Integration

The employee who begins to lose hearing usually tries first to hide the problem. Colleagues and management eventually become aware of the problem and respond by moving the person to a job where verbal communication is less important. In large companies and in government agencies, this kind of change can work well, though it requires some retraining and may entail a demotion for the employee. In smaller organizations, however, there is a good chance that the employee will be fired, even when colleagues try to intervene.

The now unemployed deafened person searches desperately for assistance, but it must be individualized, because each person's situation is different. A fifty-year-old official in Lille has a completely different set of problems from a twenty-five-year-old laborer in Alsace. People in such divergent situations cannot simply be placed in programs designed for adolescents, where most of the participants are of a similar age and level. Social service agencies are haunted by the fear of having to tailor programs, even though such individualized approaches are the only ones that will work with adults, because they cost more to operate and require more effort to organize.

Senior Citizens

With advancing age comes presbycusis, the inexorable deterioration
of the structures of the inner ear and its nerve fibers. Sometimes the
onset of presbycusis becomes noticeable in one's fifties, but occasionally much later, past the seventies. Heredity is the major determinant:
certain genetic lines have more fragile ears. The hearing loss begins
with the higher-pitched tones and is not noticeable at first. Then the
subject fails to hear the singing of the birds, perhaps, or the chiming of
the doorbell, though normal conversation presents no difficulty. From
age seventy, hearing in the entire auditory range loses sensitivity, and
auditory discrimination deteriorates in both high- and low-pitched
sounds. The subject begins to ask people to repeat words and phrases
and begins to turn up the volume on the radio and television. Family
members begin speaking louder. They also begin trying to convince
the subject to see a physician about the hearing decline. Rarely does
the subject make the decision to seek assistance. Some people, in fact,
find a kind of comfort in not being able to hear absolutely everything.
So many worthless things are said in this fast and bustling world, why
hear better when others can just speak more loudly to convey things
that are important?

Medical treatment hardly ever stops this progressive hearing loss.
A hearing aid may help, depending on the nature of the hearing loss,
but it may not. The effectiveness of the hearing aid depends also on a
range of other changes and difficulties that affect older people. For example, the memory begins to decline, along with the powers of mental concentration, making it harder to understand social situations.
The hearing-impaired person may need more time to understand spoken words. Declines in vision can reduce the efficacy of lipreading,
another aid for the hearing impaired. It becomes difficult to follow
complicated logical arguments, conversations held in rapid speech,
and discussions involving more than one or two people.

The person becomes isolated, even within the family. The subject
pays attention only to conversations addressed directly to him or her
and ignores those aimed at other persons, which seem off "in left
field" and too tiring to follow. The person may accept isolation simply
out of fatigue. Especially after retirement from paid employment, he

or she may withdraw from active life, a decision made all the easier if there is a physical disability or limitation.

And yet, this is precisely the time to act. It is very difficult to readapt to social life once it has been abandoned. The solution is not to give up. From the moment the senior citizen begins to withdraw from conversation and doesn't perceive ambient noise, the people around him or her, family and friends, must try to help sustain an active life, including conversations with others.

Unfortunately, family and friends often lack the knowledge to deal with the onset of hearing loss and even to help the person cope with the vagaries of technical aids once these are obtained. For example, senior citizens often have difficulty adjusting a hearing aid properly. The switch has a microphone position and a telephone position; the potentiometer allows one to raise or lower the output volume. To position the aid in the ear properly and to adjust the volume can be difficult if the person's fingers no longer have sufficient agility. Here is where the help of family and friends can be critical, but, too often, these people are just as ignorant of the proper techniques as the subject. Even personnel in retirement homes and other institutions usually know little or nothing about hearing aids. As a result, one often finds hearing aids tucked away in the corner of a drawer, unused, because the hearing-impaired person has become weary of making the constant adjustments or because the device was never properly fitted and the person failed to ask the specialist to make a new fitting. In this climate of indifference, the deafened senior citizen often becomes accustomed to a communication desert, particularly if the spouse is dead or there has been little family contact for some time. The subject lapses into a vegetative existence.

The treatment for such melancholy progressions into solitude must come from institutional staff and medical personnel who have experience in dealing with services for the hearing-impaired senior citizen. It will also help to integrate the hearing-impaired senior—properly fitted with a hearing aid or trained in lipreading—into small institutions that principally serve seniors who can hear, so as to provide an environment where conversation is always in the air.

Conclusion

The Future of the Dialogue

MERVIN D. GARRETSON

As we look ahead to the challenges in France and the United States, we should keep in mind the statement by Robert Louis Stevenson that the major aim in life is to be what you are, and to become all that you are capable of becoming. The Spanish philosopher Ortega y Gasset made a similar observation: "All life is the struggle, the effort to be itself."

One of the threads running through the French-American dialogue, as embodied in this colloquium, is our mutual admiration, which has continued for more than 200 years. In the United States, deaf people and professionals working with the deaf have deep and strong roots with the deaf Frenchman Laurent Clerc and his many contributions to early American education for the deaf. In a much broader sense, our affinity for France goes back to General Lafayette and the brave French forces who helped the United States to become an independent nation in 1776.

Important threads, intertwined in the education of deaf children, youth, and adults at all levels, include sign language—both American Sign Language (ASL) and French Sign Language (LSF)—the need for deaf people to be involved in all matters relating to deafness, the education of parents, bilingual and bicultural considerations, the role of interpreting, emerging technology and telecommunications, all matters of access, employment, minorities, the law, and governmental and political considerations.

Mervin D. Garretson is president of the Commission on Pedagogy, World Federation of the Deaf.

The following are some of the concerns and needs expressed during our conference:

1. Continued exploration of the meaning of deafness above and beyond the medical or pathological perception of deaf persons as guinea pigs, objects of research, and people in need of remediation. Rather, deafness needs to be viewed within a social, cultural, and linguistic context. What is involved in deaf culture? Who makes up the total deaf population? What about people who become deaf in their early or late teens? People who become deaf after retirement? Is there a "variable" deaf culture? We must avoid stereotyping—not all deaf people are the same or even use the same communication mode. Even so, many of these people are active members of the deaf community.

2. Sign languages vis-à-vis spoken languages. Does the national spoken, printed, and written language of each country have a discernible impact on its sign language? Should future studies focus on sign language (both LSF and ASL) within a broader context?

3. The crucial importance of educational placement options— both in residential or special schools and in mainstreamed (integrated) school situations. We need to take a close look at what I call "the unwritten curriculum." Of the 365 days in a year, we spend only approximately 10 percent of this time in a classroom. Almost all of our education, whether we are deaf or hearing, takes place in the 90 percent of the time we are out of the classroom. What are the implications for children who do not hear and do not have general access to information and language in a regular public school setting?

A number of more specific recommendations emerged from our conference, including the establishment of a structure for future collaboration. Scientific committees and future French and American moderators might be charged with the responsibility for developing a prioritized list of projects. This group would communicate through correspondence and meetings in each country and work with the two sponsoring foundations—the French-American Foundation and the Fondation Franco-Américaine—to advance a common agenda.

The problem of teacher training in France needs to be addressed. At the present time, no provisions have been made in France to prepare either deaf or hearing teachers in the specific field of education of the deaf. Perhaps French teachers could obtain degrees in education of the deaf from Gallaudet University, using the Gallaudet-Philippines program as a model. This would require French acceptance of the American certificate and the cooperation of a French educational institution. Another approach might be the establishment of a Gallaudet University extension center in a French university, as at the universities of Costa Rica and Puerto Rico.

The World Federation of the Deaf has expressed interest in more international deaf youth leadership training programs. The International Center at Gallaudet University has been involved in leadership training programs for several years and has developed materials and program models that could be utilized to develop a French-American young leaders training seminar for individuals between the ages of twenty and thirty. Another possibility is a youth exchange, which could be initiated by inviting a group of young French teenagers to attend the month-long summer camp of the National Association of the Deaf (NAD) on the West Coast of the United States. This leadership camp, which has been in operation for a number of years, provides a comprehensive training program, including survival skills, talks from outstanding deaf and hearing individuals in the field, hands-on experience at editing a daily newspaper, and many other activities.

Videotapes of this colloquium need to be widely disseminated in both countries. Videotapes should also be distributed of the 1989 Deaf Way conference held in Washington, D.C., with 6,000 participants from over eighty countries, which accentuated the positive aspects of deafness.

French policymakers, government officials, and regulators should be invited to visit the United States for an official tour of local, state, and federally supported programs for deaf children as well as private institutions. All types of educational programming would be observed—residential, day, and mainstreamed placements.

Arrangements for exchange teachers should be considered so that American educators could observe bilingual/bicultural education approaches in France; French teachers would have an opportunity to do the same in the United States with programs experimenting with this philosophy, where the "native" sign language becomes the primary language for instruction, with the spoken language of the country taught as a second language. Cultural aspects of deafness would also be an intrinsic part of the curriculum. There is a need for a cross-cultural study of the extent of such bilingual education in the two countries in a search for comparative results. Several universities might be approached to undertake this project.

Museum educators in the United States could be invited to observe some of the cultural interpretation programs in France, such as at La Villette, that employ deaf animators and guides. Similarly, French museum personnel may wish to visit U.S. national parks and other sites that provide deaf guides and interpreter services. One recommendation was that Guy Bouchauveau might spend time in American museums training deaf museum educators and making a presentation at a meeting of the American Association of Museums. Such a collaboration might be brought about through Dr. Deborah Sonnenstrahl of Gallaudet University, a deaf expert on such presentations.

The conference participants recognized the need for a regular series of French-American meetings, the next to be held in the United States. Planners of the next meeting should develop a specific agenda that would focus on a selected number of mutual problems. Among agenda items would be the training of interpreters in the translation of English to LSF and French to ASL; discussions about the potential for developing a common archive of deaf history, in particular, a visual archive; planning for a retreat that would join policymakers and government officials with leaders of the deaf community in both countries; and planning for a French-American meeting of leaders of advocacy groups to share techniques for contact with legislators, government officials, and public educators.

Finally, educators, deaf leaders, and service providers from both countries need to take a meaningful and realistic look into the years ahead. What does the future hold for tomorrow's deaf children? More important to us at the moment, what does the future hold for today's deaf children who will soon become adults? We must not engage in planned obsolescence. Years ago the American writer and historian Henry Adams complained that Harvard prepared him for life in the eighteenth century. He had to spend the rest of his life trying to catch up with the nineteenth century and to anticipate the twentieth!

With advancing and rapidly changing medicine and technology, tomorrow's milieu for the deaf and hard of hearing will be much different from today's. Are we preparing our children for a world that no longer exists? We need to consider the deaf person of today, of the next ten years, and beyond. Deaf people have values relating to both deaf and hearing cultures, and both languages, ASL and English, LSF and French. Deaf people live in a real world, not one that is evanescent. We will continue to seek, meet, and deal with everyday realities, and, certainly, with the help and understanding of these two foundations, we will succeed.

Index

Abbou, Marie-Thérèse, 216
Academy of French Sign Language
    (ALSF), 136, 137
Adams, Henry, 255
Adepoju, Gabriel, 173
adult-onset hearing loss. *See* late-
    deafened persons
ALDA. *See* Association of Late Deaf-
    ened Adults
Alexander, Lamar, 184
AMERICA 2000, 184, 188
American School for the Deaf, 31
American Sign Language (ASL), 4,
    42; acknowledged as language, 15,
    98; curriculum for, 131–135; as lan-
    guage of instruction, 124; poetry
    in, 210; as political issue, 98–102;
    teaching of, 118, 119, 131–135; of,
    use in BiBi philosophy, 121, 124,
    125, 128. *See also* interpreters for
    the deaf
Americans with Disabilities Act
    (ADA), 153, 184, 187–188, 225
Anderson, Glenn, 172, 176
Andersson, Yerker, 173–174
ANFIDA. *See* National Association
    of Interpreters for the Hearing-
    Impaired
ANILS. *See* National Association of
    Sign Language Interpreters
ANPEDA. *See* National Association
    of Parents of Hearing-Impaired
    Children

ANPILS. *See* National Association for
    Interpretation in Sign Language
ASL. *See* American Sign Language
assistive listening devices (ALDs), 239
Association for the Creation of Funds
    for Deafness (ACFOS), 192
Association of Black Professionals in
    Deafness, 175
Association of College Educators in
    Hearing Impairment, 100
Association of Late Deafened Adults
    (ALDA), 239, 240

Babbidge Report, 185
Baudot code, 226
Belissen, Patrick, 4
Berge, Françoise, 204
bilingual/bicultural approach (BiBi),
    118–119, 121–130; components of,
    124–126; spirit of, 127–130
bilingual communication, 28, 47, 52,
    69, 112; in LSF classes, 140–143,
    144–146
Borel-Maisonny gestures, 111
Bossuet School, 137
Bouchauveau, Guy, 254
Bouvet, Danielle, 216
Bowe, Frank, 176
Brusque, Martine, 29
BUCODES. *See* Coordination Bureau
    of Associations of the Late-
    Deafened and Hearing Impaired
Burnham, Daniel, 32

257

French Sign Language (*continued*)
52; plays performed in, 16, 217;
teaching of, 110, 111–112, 136–139,
140–143. *See also* interpreters for
the deaf

Gallaudet, Thomas Hopkins, 7, 30–31,
53, 184–185
Gallaudet University, 31, 32, 33, 43,
53, 58, 100, 152, 178, 185, 186, 253;
"Deaf President Now" movement
at, 101
Galloway, Gertrude, 5
GESTES. *See* Expert Study Group on
Therapy and Deafness
Greater Los Angeles Council on Deaf-
ness, Inc. (GLAD), 195–196
Grégoire, Abbé, 10, 11
Guiblets School, 137

Hairston, Ernest, 176
Humphries, Tom, 16

IDEA. *See* Individuals with Disabilities
Education Act
Indiana School for the Deaf, 116–117,
118–119, 123
Individuals with Disabilities Education
Act (IDEA), 42, 103, 186, 188. *See
also* Education for All Handicapped
Children Act of 1975
International Visual Theater (IVT),
136, 137, 204, 217
interpreters for the deaf, 41–42, 63–
75; certification of, 66–68, 71–73;
in criminal cases, 80–91; in France,
76–79; in mental health care, 207;
in museums, 218–219, 254; quality
of, 74–75; role of, 68–70; in the
theater, 213, 217–218; training of,
65–66, 73
Itard, Jean-Marc, 11

Johnson, Lyndon, 185
Jordan, I. King, 16, 43
Jouannic, Father, 136

Kannapell, Barbara, 16, 57
Kendall Demonstration Elementary
School (at Gallaudet University),
185

Laborit, Emmanuelle, 17
Langue des Signes Françaises (LSF),
See French Sign Language
late-deafened persons: employment
for, 245; psychological aspects, 51,
243–245; rehabilitation assistance
for, 236–238, 241; self-help groups
for, 238–240, 241; senior citizens
as, 246–247; in the U.S., 235–241
legislation affecting deaf people, 153–
157, 160, 184, 186, 187–188, 192
Lentz, Ella Mae, 133
Les Enfants du Silence, 17
Liaison and Action Committee of
Parents of Children and Adults Suffering from Multiple Disabilities
(CLAPEAHA), 51
Lincoln, Abraham, 185
lipreading, 244–245, 246
"Love Is Never Silent," 212
LSF. *See* French Sign Language

mainstreaming, in France, 191; in the
U.S., 27, 28, 104–105
Markowicz, Harry, 16
Massieu, Jean, 30
Matlin, Marlee, 212
Mayes, Tom, 16
Mba, Peter, 173
Mead, Margaret, 33
Medico-Social Centers of Preschool
Action (CAMSPs), 109
mental health care for deaf people,
200; in France, 202–207
Mercurio, Jean-François, 5
Merrill, Edward C., Jr., 176
"Mes Mains Ont la Parole," 216
Meyer, Marcella, 4
Mikos, Ken, 133
Mimoun, Rachid, 4
Minitel terminals, 51, 54, 228–232
minority deaf people, 170–179